MARRIA

H4409

ETHICS

OUR

CHOICES

Series editor

Canon Stephen Platten

The series aims to introduce specific subjects of concern and controversy within Christian ethics to a wide variety of readers. Each subject is approached at a serious level, but technical language is avoided. Each book should appeal to a wide readership and will be useful in introductory seminary programmes, in programmes for congregational development, and also to individuals seeking information and guidance within their Christian life.

Canon Stephen Platten is the Archbishop of Canterbury's Secretary for Ecumenical Affairs, and Co-Secretary of the Anglican–Roman Catholic International Commission. Previously he was at the Anglican Cathedral in Portsmouth and taught ethics for five years at the Lincoln theological college; he was also Chief Examiner in Ethics for the General Ministerial Examination of the Church of England. He has published in a number of learned journals including *Theology* and the *Anglican Theological Review*. He was Chairman of the Society for the Study of Christian Ethics at its inception, and has been responsible for forging the very close links which exist between that Society and the Society for Christian Ethics in North America.

Already published
Marriage Helen Oppenheimer
Good for the Poor Michael Taylor

Planned titles in the series include
The Morality of Power David Attwood
Women and Ethics Janet Soskice

MARRIAGE

Helen Oppenheimer

MOWBRAY

Mowbray
A Cassell imprint
Villiers House, 41/47 Strand, London WC2N 5JE, England

First published 1990

British Library Cataloguing in Publication Data
Oppenheimer, Helen, *1926–*
    Marriage.—(Ethics: our choices)
    1 Marriage—Christian viewpoints
    I Title   II Series
    261.8'3581

ISBN 0–264–67193–7

Typeset by Colset Pte Ltd, Singapore
Printed and bound in Great Britain by
Biddles Ltd, Guildford and King's Lynn

Contents

Editor's foreword

'The Brangwens shrank from applying their religion to their own immediate actions. They wanted the sense of the eternal and the immortal, not a list of rules for everyday conduct' (D. H. Lawrence, *The Rainbow*). In these two sentences are encapsulated so many of the questions which continue to dominate Christian thought on moral issues. Must Christianity necessarily require of people specific moral responses? Is there a distinctive Christian ethic? How can wider reflections on doctrine be effectively integrated within Christian moral thought? Issues like these and a number of others will be addressed in this series of books, as we focus, one by one, on a number of topical ethical questions.

A variety of different stimuli converge upon individuals and communities to press home these questions with continuing force at the present time. Technological advancement and medical research both mean that the empirical data with which we must deal in our moral lives change swiftly and often. The increasing diversity of most Western cultures, where many religions, and none, jostle alongside each other, calls out of the moral agent discernment of what his or her religious convictions demand in such a complex world. Changing gender roles and women's issues raise another set of moral challenges. Shifting political attitudes, both internationally (especially within the Eastern bloc) and within nations, contribute yet further patterns of what we might call moral vectors. All of these factors mean that ethical issues are being debated with more liveliness than ever. The multiplication of introductory books on Christian moral theory is a function of this accelerating interest.

In this volume on marriage, Helen Oppenheimer engages with many of these issues with the clarity and gracefulness of style for which she has become so well known. Her approach stands within the continuing stream of Christian humanism. She begins with the highest aspirations within human culture. These she affirms and then takes as the basis for a sophisticated but never arcane series of reflections from a Christian standpoint. Controversy is not avoided and there is an independence of thought which will challenge us to rethink our conventional attitudes. The Brangwens would not have been disappointed.

Stephen Platten

Preface

This book began with the notion of revising and bringing up to date *The Marriage Bond*, published by Faith Press in 1976 and now out of print. I am particularly grateful to Canon Stephen Platten for suggesting a more positive undertaking, by asking me to write for this series; and for all the help and encouragement he has given me along the way. His comments have been truly constructive, especially in pointing out to me places where my argument had become too compressed.

The upshot is an almost new book, with a few paragraphs and turns of phrase from *The Marriage Bond* embedded in it and indicated in the notes. I have also included, by kind permission, most of my Mary Sumner Lecture on 'Fidelity' given for the Mothers' Union in 1978 and published by them; and a good deal of a paper on 'The authority of the New Testament in ethics' given to the Society for the Study of Christian Ethics in 1983 and published in *The Modern Churchman* (XXVI, No. 4).

Professor Brenda Hoggett of the Law Commission was so kind as to send me a copy of their Discussion Paper on the law of divorce, *Facing the Future*, and ask for comments. Most of my reply has become Chapter 8 and the Appendix. I am very grateful to Professor Hoggett for her friendly response which has helped me to clarify my final draft at some points.

The beginning of Chapter 12 is adapted from a paper I originally wrote for a small working party on education in personal relationships, which met under the auspices of the C. of E. Boards of Education and Social Responsibility. I have also made use of two talks I gave to clergy at Dinton House near Salisbury, with Canon Ian Dunlop as my host on a most agreeable occasion.

One's thoughts develop gradually over the years and the situations to which they need to be applied are certainly not static. Not recantations but fresh emphases and refurbished explanations keep on becoming necessary. The long-standing problems about divorce and remarriage, with which *The Marriage Bond* was mainly concerned, are still there and have not been settled; but more drastic questions about the meaning and value of marriage itself now occupy the foreground.

Many of my debts will be obvious: particularly, as ever, to my husband. I hope too that my abiding gratefulness to my parents will be evident. I should like to mention my gratitude to all the other members of the Church of England working party on the law of marriage, whose report (1988) is called *An Honourable Estate*. I should also like to thank Mrs Cecily Ilbert for helping me to take seriously some arguments I had underestimated. Other people to whom I owe a great deal for much appreciated encouragement and friendly discussion are Professor G. R. Dunstan, Professor Emeritus of King's College London; Father Clement Mullenger, SSM; and Professor Philip Turner of the General Theological Seminary, New York. I also owe a long-standing debt to my Oxford philosophy tutor, Mrs Martha Kneale, not least for saying when I told her long ago that I was engaged to be married, 'You won't find it will interfere with work. It will make it all more interesting.'

Helen Oppenheimer
August 1989

To Margaret
and in memory of aj.

– 1 –

Where are we?

Before this strange disease of modern life,
With its sick hurry, its divided aims,
Its heads o'ertax'd, its palsied hearts, was rife . . .

Matthew Arnold, *The Scholar Gipsy* (1853)

FEARS

It would be a brave person who would say that the institution of marriage is in an admirable state today. On the one hand we have people complaining about the loss of Christian standards. Marriage is meant to be permanent, faithful and harmonious; and we can see for ourselves how often it is nothing of the kind. Divorce has now become socially acceptable; cohabitation is no longer thought of as 'fornication'; promiscuity is blatant. The notion of 'moral effort' has an old-fashioned sound about it now. Instant gratification is claimed as a kind of human right. It is no wonder that moralists are rushing to conclude that our old values are in the mud.

On the other hand we have a different set of complaints: that marriage is a straitjacket and an excuse for hypocrisy; that our 'high standards' are a tyranny; that the old values of family life have been merely a licence for the strong to oppress the weak; that people must choose worthwhile ways of life for themselves and we should get rid of the taboos which discourage them.

The two sets of complaints are not directly engaged in battle with one another, but anyone who wants to be liberal-minded and to listen to what our contemporaries are really saying will feel beset on both sides, fighting on two fronts, forced on to the defensive one way or the other or maybe both. Is it merely starry-eyed to take a positive view in these circumstances?

Christians can at least start with a solid basis of agreement between traditional affirmations and what marriage still is in law. Canon B30 of the Church of England 'affirms, according to our Lord's teaching, that marriage is in its nature a union permanent and lifelong, for better for worse, till death do them part, of one

1

man with one woman'. The law of England concurs. In every register office there is a notice informing all who come that marriage is a voluntary union for life of one man and one woman. What more can we ask?

Realists must be uncomfortably aware of how theory and practice can diverge. Marriage 'in its nature' is permanent and life-long: but it looks as if it is crumbling all around us. The law says that marriage is a union for life, but it makes provision for its ending practically on demand. It is said that one in three marriages now come to grief and it is gloomily forecast that soon it will be one in two.

People who prophesy so are apt to forget that one likely way to make something happen, especially when it is something unde-sirable, is to keep anticipating it. 'I shall fail.' 'Everything is going wrong.' 'Nobody cares.' These announcements are character-istically self-fulfilling. It is worth remembering that the divorce statistics do not have the status of a fixed doom that we can only accept. There is something more open-ended than that about them.

We could almost say that there is no such thing as *the* divorce rate. Suppose we assert that one in three marriages at present ends in divorce. It sounds as if we are doing something like giving the accident rate of marriages, as we might give the accident rate of journeys by car or aeroplane. But marriages are journeys which go on for years. Here are two people in the midst of the upheaval of divorce. With which unbroken marriages is theirs to be compared? Marriages which are breaking now may have begun twenty years ago, or last year. The brides and bridegrooms cutting their wedding cakes today will develop their own divorce rates, and we shall not know what these will be until some of them have had their golden weddings. There is time to help or hinder, and certainly no need to stand about wringing our hands.

HOPES

If we would like to help, we have to look at the facts with accuracy and balance. In particular, it is as well to be quite counter-suggestible about the notion that there was once a golden age which has now departed from us. To look back with nostalgia to the past, especially to a past which never really existed, is no way to understand the complexities of the significant changes of our late twentieth-century world.

There is a tendency among Christians to get both our pessimism and our optimism wrong. We have a mental picture of what marriage and the family ought to be like, we suppose it goes back to time immemorial, and we fear it is now being destroyed; but we hope that if we hold fast we can revive it in its lost glory. This picture is constantly being refuted. For example, it was well refuted a quarter of a century ago by two vigorous paperbacks which came out at the same time by a Christian and a non-Christian, G. R. Dunstan[1] and Ronald Fletcher,[2] both showing in different ways that the Golden Age never existed, and that the way events had moved was encouraging, not discouraging, for marriage and family life. Their statistics are now out of date but their converging emphasis is worth recalling, both by those who can remember what 'the sixties' were really like and by those increasing numbers for whom that decade merely symbolizes situation ethics and getting rid of structures.

There are plenty of newer books and pamphlets which can fill in the picture since then, good and bad, in serious but lively detail. For example, the Study Commission on the Family has produced an admirable series of booklets full of information about what marriage and family life really are like today. From the whole complicated story two facts particularly need to be emphasized, both challenges not disasters, putting a strain on marriage by their life-enhancing promise.

First, people are living longer. Marriages have the chance to go on for many years, long after the children have grown up. 'Till death us do part' has become the remote contingency, not a likelihood to be lived with daily. So we have old risks taking new forms. Broken homes and remarriages, lone parents, step-parents and step-children, are not new notions, products of our modern instability. Old churchyards and old stories are full of them. But today it is apt to be divorce that is the marriage breaker, whether we believe that people bring it upon themselves or succumb to an unkind fate. Death is more likely to hold back and let people see their children's children and even their great-grandchildren. In this respect the golden age is now. But it is no wonder that for good and ill husbands and wives, operating on a longer time-scale, demand more of each other. Once people were young and then old, but now they may hope for many years of being middle-aged. When they have brought up a family but failed to achieve the harmony they once hoped for, 'marriage is for life' could sound like a life sentence with no remission. There is bound to be more pressure to escape from it.

Second, it is hard to overestimate the difference that reliable birth control has made. The point is not either to defend or attack the 'permissive society', still less to talk, as one was invited to do in the 1960s, about a 'new morality'. What is new is our terms of reference, the conditions in which our morality has to be applied. In

3

the 'olden days' people generally had to put up with life as they found it. For a woman, marriage meant child-bearing and rearing; to stay single meant either celibacy or ruin. In both marriage and the single life there could be deep satisfactions, but the people most likely to find these were the people lucky enough to have contented natures. There were fewer life-shaping choices available in everyday life.

But now women are able to aspire to do what was impossible for them before, take charge of their own lives. The fact that these hopes are still only partially fulfilled may make them more poignant but not less strong. Because women can plan their families, anyway negatively, they now have lively expectations of entering into the human world of jobs and ambition and vocation, without thereby renouncing the human worlds of romantic love and the bringing up of children. They need less restrictive protection, and their remaining vulnerability is for a smaller proportion of their lives.

Yet some Christians seem unable to consider that 'new occasions' actually might 'teach new duties', as the hymn they sang quite heartily in their youth gave them warning. It is all very well to preach about God's unchanging will: but it is odd to ascribe to God an inflexibility when circumstances change which would be no virtue in human beings.

But perhaps it is not so odd that to some people the real risks of changing circumstances will always seem to outweigh the advantages. Human life does not get less perilous, though the perils alter. The pressure that marriage is under today is the pressure of high expectations demanding to be satisfied. As longevity has given marriages time, contraception gives them space: both to develop, and to feel strains. When women's lives were inexorably filled with bearing and rearing children it might never become apparent if spouses after all had very little in common. There was no room for their personal relationship to be, or to fail to be, the meaning of their lives.

Though the past was no golden age, the present time is certainly not wonderfully easy to live in. The defeat of great expectations is more desolating than troubles one had reckoned to be part of the human condition. Might-have-beens are more cruel than expected hardships. People who have the advantage of not being worn down by their physical circumstances may still be haunted by the anxiety that the choices they have been able to make have been unsatisfactory. Increasingly, in the next generation, the children of people who have been free to consider their own happiness, but have not always found it, will have the weight of their parents' problems around their own necks.

CHRISTIAN UNDERSTANDING?

What is the Christian church to do in all this? We may well reply 'repent', but of what? More than of moral laxity, it is time to repent of the kind of nagging self-righteousness which drives other people into laxity. Its name is 'Pharisaism', except that this might not be very fair to the historical Pharisees. When moralists nag, ordinary human beings lose heart. There seems no point in being good when goodness is so difficult, and not only difficult but unattractive. Who wants to be like the sort of Christian who is always worrying about 'standards' and seems to have lost sight of people? When the Church appears to forget that morality is about people and their joys and sorrows and what is truly good for them, it is no wonder that so many of our contemporaries expect no understanding from the Church, either of what makes them happy, their hopes and plans, or of what they fear and what worries and miseries they are going through.

But inadequate understanding is not altogether surprising either. When church people feel out of their depth and battered by the complexities of modern life, they readily take refuge in the notion that many of the sufferers claiming our sympathy have brought their troubles upon their own heads. As Browning's Childe Roland put it, they 'must be wicked to deserve such pain'. It makes problems seem less distressing if we can tell ourselves that the misery might have been averted if people had really tried.

Especially when a large social problem such as widespread breakdown of marriage is in question, disapproval has seemed the easiest way of sorting out one's confused moral ideas. So Christians who deplore divorce too simplistically think of it as if it were an attractive alternative which unregenerate human beings wilfully choose, although they know it is forbidden. It is apparent, of course, that divorce is horrible for children, but good people have too often talked as if the adults rather liked it.

This misconception is beginning to collapse. There is hope in the fact that many people, not only Christians, and including young married people, are seeing the real point. When friends or relatives are divorced it becomes apparent what a miserable experience it is apt to be for all concerned. Divorce is not a positive and exciting upheaval like moving house, which may be exhausting and quite a wrench but is fundamentally constructive. Divorce is not an adventure which for some reason the churches are against. It is more like a kind of bereavement or amputation, painful and traumatic, at best a 'merciful release'.

Part of the problem is the difficulty Christians seem to have in thinking about God's will in a positive way. Human beings are apt to want what they are not allowed to have. So when they are told that divorce is wrong it appears as forbidden fruit, something to set one's heart upon. But we know that it is not good for us to have everything we want, so divorce must be made as hard as possible and unhappily married people must just struggle on and be faithful in adversity.

This is a disastrous caricature of Christian teaching on marriage. The God Christ taught us to believe in is not a killjoy who wants to spoil human pleasure, who would rather we went through misery just to strengthen our characters, who gives us laws to see whether we will obey them or not. On the contrary, the Gospels are full of treasures and rewards, worth anything to win. Obedience should not be a dreary denial of what we want, but an enthusiastic grasp of what we find we really do want. Sin is not doing what we enjoy and then finding that God was watching us all along and is about to punish us, but missing the point and turning our backs on happiness. Faith is not keeping pointless rules but holding on loyally to the idea that there really is a point which will appear in due course. If Christians lose this characteristic vision they are left with the false gospel which is called moralism, consisting of prohibitions and permissions rather than promises. It has to be admitted that moralism in this sense has been especially prevalent in matters of sex and marriage.

Religious people are sometimes inclined to look at human life and see what they expect to see, selfishness and disobedience. So they take the partial truth for the whole truth, and preach a gospel of unselfishness and obedience, in which Christians have nothing to do but deny themselves and the good life is all giving and no taking. The austerity of this is bound to arouse opposition. Why should God's children not be happy? So permissive morality feeds off the morality of self-abnegation. The split between rigorists and liberals widens. It needs to be noticed that often liberals do not get away from moralism either: they simply emphasize permissions rather than prohibitions. 'Yes, you may have a divorce' or 'Yes, you may live together before marriage'. The message is 'God won't mind' instead of 'God will be angry'.

Liberalism and rigorism about marriage are both, in their different ways, between the Charybdis of smugness and the Scylla of defeatism. The smugness of liberalism takes the form: 'We don't need all these shackles any more. Let adult people shape their own lives.' The defeatism of liberalism is the bitter affirmation that 'marriage is a con' and family life is a trap. The contrary defeatism of rigorism is the conviction that values are collapsing all around us and that we must desperately try to uphold standards. The smugness easily takes over: in *Christian* marriage we have a fortress against the tempest.

– 2 –

The pairbond

Between husband and wife friendship seems to exist by nature.

Aristotle, *Ethics*

FROM THE BEGINNING

It would be odd if Christians were really supposed to shut themselves up in a fortress and leave the world outside. It should be more characteristic of them to have something to offer to the world. But if they are to be able to make their best insights more available, it is high time to get out of the bad habit of talking about 'Christian marriage'. The Root report, *Marriage, Divorce and the Church*,[1] was right to take seriously the exact wording of its terms of reference: 'to prepare a statement of the Christian doctrine of marriage', not 'the doctrine of Christian marriage'. The importance of this distinction has become greater not less since that report was written. It would be harshly paradoxical to deny outright that there is such a thing as Christian marriage, but the denial could be a justifiable corrective to the kind of monopolizing take-over bid which believers are too apt to feel that they ought to try to make.

Some of the best Christian insights about marriage are expressed in the Form of Solemnization of Matrimony in the Book of Common Prayer. Marriage, the priest is to affirm at the outset, 'is an honourable estate, instituted of God in the time of man's innocency'. In more modern language, this means that what Christians enter into today when they marry is much older than the Gospel and goes back to the origins of human existence. Christ did not institute marriage. He 'adorned and beautified' it 'with his presence'. So it is fair to take the wedding at Cana of Galilee as an especially clear example of a marriage blessed by God: the wedding of two people who had never heard of Christianity, whose laws and customs concerning marriage and divorce were untouched by the teaching of Christ. If we could set out all their assumptions, many priests today would surely have reservations about marrying them. Yet any doubts we have about the story fasten upon the miracle, not

8

upon the gracious presence of the Lord at such a wedding.

There is no need for Christians to be possessive about marriage. At least they can start in the same place as everyone else, with the tendency of human beings to form 'pairbonds'. This simply is a fact about the human species, however complicated the detailed history becomes. Humanity, said Aristotle, 'is naturally disposed to pairing. . . . Human beings live together not only for the sake of reproduction but also for the various purposes of life'. As Mary Midgley put it in *Beast and Man: the roots of human nature*: 'Individuals want to live in pairs before they have any children, and continue to do so when their children have gone'.[2] She adds in a footnote:

People who think that our species has no natural pair-forming tendency should look in detail at how life goes on in species that actually do not have it, such as chimps. *No social consequences* at all follow mating; all males present mate any female in season (unless she rejects one or two), and everyone walks off afterward to live just as they did before. People are not like this anywhere, any more than wolves or geese.[3]

We should not look at the pairbond through rose-coloured spectacles, but the point is that the notion of faithful monogamous marriage is not the kind of vague and unrealistic ideal that never comes down from the clouds to touch earth: on the contrary, it is rooted in human experience. If faithfulness in marriage is a law, it is a law which latches on to our nature. If God commands it, He commands it because it suits us.

The point is as biblical as any fundamentalist could wish.

From the beginning of creation, 'God made them male and female'. 'For this reason a man shall leave his father and mother and be joined to his wife, and the two shall become one.'[4]

That is the Lord, in St Mark's Gospel, quoting from the Book of Genesis. It is indeed the most basic Christian belief about marriage. We can take it as authoritative without being fundamentalist at all. In affirming that the marriage union belongs to human nature we are going back to the roots of our tradition which has developed in the way it has because our forebears were trying, under God, to make sense of our human experience.

There is no conflict between religion and science here. It is not only theologians but palaeontologists who trace the pairbond right back to our origins. We do not have to be convinced that the names of the first married couple were Adam and Eve in order to attend to the idea that the 'one-flesh' union is part of God's purpose for man and woman. Nor on the other hand need we take as sacrosanct all the theories of the people who study early hominid bones, to find illumination about what human beings are from the way they seem to have evolved.

There is a female skeleton called Lucy, over three-and-a-half million years old, found in Ethiopia in 1974, remarkable for her completeness. Nearly half the bones are there, enough for the whole to be deduced. Lucy is not human. She is a kind of hominid who has been classified as *Australopithecus afarensis*. She had an apelike head and a small brain. The point is that she sets a problem. Her finder, Donald C. Johanson, in a fascinating popular book called *Lucy: The Beginnings of Humankind*,[5] makes much of the fact that, without being especially intelligent, she had a remarkably human-shaped body and walked upright.

There used to be a notion that 'man' developed a large brain and then rose on to his feet so as to free his hands to use tools; but Lucy seemingly did nothing of the kind. No tools have been found earlier than a million years after she walked and ran about. Yet walking upright is not particularly useful in itself. Running four-footed is on the whole a more efficient way of getting about. The answer must lie in a whole way of life.

In one chapter of his book[6] Dr Johanson develops a complex argument that Lucy's way of life was family life: in other words that the family lies further back in our origins than our brainpower. He draws the contrast with apes, who though sociable creatures fend entirely for themselves. They do not bring food to one another and have no idea of pairbonding. A mother will bring up one child at a time, and the child will cling on to her so that there is no need for free hands. But if childhood is to be prolonged and there are still to be enough young to continue the race, a mother must look after more than one child at a time. So she needs help: a mate who is able both to use his hands to bring her food and also to distinguish her from the other females and in some way be concerned for her in particular. Lucy suggests the beginning of this development. Pair-bonding of course is not exclusive to human beings, but we can say that it is characteristically human, an integral part of our evolution. Tentatively we can add that our significant individuality seems to go far back, as far back as we can trace human origins.

It is an attractive thought that the spouse is older than the technician, even that our distinctive humanity has something to do with relationships not just with cleverness. It would be rash to put too much on the neatness of a particular theory, and of course one cannot derive exclusive lifelong monogamy from reading about *Australopithecus afarensis*; but perhaps one might be ready to extend the ancient maxim 'nothing human can be alien to me'[7] to 'nothing hominid can be alien to me'.

HONOURABLE ESTATE

The notion that marriage is best understood in terms of human pair-bonding has a considerable appeal, as a good corrective to the notions that marriage is no more than a licence for otherwise sinful sexuality, and that it is rather deplorable that the Creator has seen fit to arrange for His world to be populated in this way. But is this new-found positive emphasis any more than a face-saving afterthought, thought up belatedly now that the negative views have become thoroughly unfashionable?

Let it be said that the negative views never had it all their own way. It is not true that until the twentieth century marriage was no more than a legalistic contract for the production and rearing of offspring. Of course people tend to find what they look for, in history as in the world around them. If one wants to believe, whether as a conservative or as a radical, that everything in our century is quite different from what has gone before, one can look at the marriages of our forebears in that light. But if one expects to see continuity as well as change, there are glimpses to be found of assumptions one can understand. Not only male dominance of women, making use of their beauty or fertility, but real mutual affection seems to be portrayed in some works of art from the ancient world depicting married couples: for instance, the throne of Tutankhamun in the Cairo museum, where a loving gesture seems to come through the conventional pose of the young king and his queen; or some of the Etruscan tombstones of husbands and wives, especially a particularly fine large one in the Villa Giulia in Rome.

Nor is the history of our own tradition as negative as it can be made to appear. There is romance, not only pious parenthood, in the Bible. 'Jacob served seven years for Rachel, and they seemed to him but a few days because of the love he had for her.'[8] When Hannah, who was to be the mother of Samuel, was distressed because she was barren, her husband tried to comfort her: 'Hannah, why do you weep? And why do you not eat? And why is your heart sad? Am I not more to you than ten sons?'[9] The Song of Songs is increasingly coming into its own as a collection of truly secular love songs.

Eastern Orthodox Christianity has been more positive and less legalistic in its appreciation of marriage than the West, with a less

11

gloomy estimate of sexuality and more emphasis on love rather than only progeny as the purpose of the union of a man and a woman.[10] St John Chrysostom said:

From the beginning God in his providence has planned this union of man and woman, and has spoken of the two as one.[11] . . . There is no influence more powerful than the bond of love, especially for husband and wife.[12]

Nor is the Western tradition entirely about marital rights, property and child-bearing. Nobody, for instance, could suppose that our English forebears were wholly uninterested in relationship in the light of Sir Henry Wotton's touching verse 'Upon the death of Sir Albert Morton's wife':

> He first deceased; she for a little tried
> To live without him, liked it not, and died.

One more example may be given because it gives a different picture of the much-maligned Victorians. It comes from the life of the great Sanskrit scholar Max Müller by his enthusiastic but objective Indian biographer Nirad C. Chaudhuri. He tells, as a piece of social history, the romantic story of Max Müller's love for Georgina Grenfell, the separation of the young people by her disapproving family, their faithfulness and their eventual happy union. His comment is that in the nineteenth century three trends converged: 'the Protestant rehabilitation of marriage; the romantic glorification of sexual love; and the Victorian transformation of the love of the Romantic Movement into married love'.[13] The Victorians, says Chaudhuri, were 'stodgy in their moralizing but not in their love-making'.[14] It is the twentieth century which has lost this 'idea of love which finds permanence in marriage without losing its intensity'.[15]

These assorted and anecdotal examples of marriage as pairbond in earlier times are given, not to maintain that everything in the garden has always been lovely, nor to belittle the real progress that has been made lately in understanding the dynamics of the way human beings relate to one another, but to correct an unconstructive split by practising a kind of inter-century ecumenism. Ancient and modern emphases have tended to lose touch with one another, to the impoverishment of both. The Christian Church has seen itself as the guardian of a fine tradition of stability and fidelity, and has paid the price by a kind of hardening of the arteries which has made Christians less ready to appreciate twentieth-century insights. So secularists concerned with human happiness have found it too easy to write off the Church as out of date, and sometimes the ideas of stability and fidelity with it. But if the new emphases on human beings in relation to one another can be seen as fresh rather than as revolutionary, the old tradition can be enlivened rather than invalidated.

A KIND OF NORM

The Christian Church neither has nor claims to have a monopoly of 'holy matrimony'. To make this plain is not to underestimate either the Gospel or the marriage union. On the contrary, the hope is to be able to understand what it means for a man and a woman to become one, in a way which will be both more Christian and more human. The word we need, though it has to be handled with care, is 'norm'. A norm is a useful link between 'ought' and 'is'. It suggests a law to be kept and at the same time the plain ordinariness of keeping it. The reason for care is that norms can too easily become tyrannical. They may seem to impose aggressive notions about 'normality'. At worst, talk about marriage as a norm may suggest that to fail in marriage is abnormal, or even that all normal human beings marry. Any such idea is miles away from the useful concept of marriage as a human norm, widespread and everyday and also life-shaping. We might prefer to call marriage a recurrent 'pattern' in human life, provided that pattern indicates a sort of lucid structure to be found emerging from the facts, not just a model people may like to follow like a knitting pattern. The notion to avoid is that marriage is really an 'ideal'.

Some people find the suggestion tempting that 'ideal' is the right word for true marriage, in the hope of getting away from the moralistic world of prohibitions and the equally moralistic world of permissions. They suggest, for instance, that Christ was 'not legislating' but giving us an ideal to follow. The trouble with this kind of ideal is not that it becomes tyrannical, but quite the contrary, that it has a tendency to remain optional. It takes somebody rather special to have an ideal and truly follow it. For most of us, an ideal is something we should like to follow but hardly ever do, something which would be realized in a perfect world but certainly not in this one. A norm or pattern on the other hand is something really to be found, quite often, in human life.

There is no reason why, if we think of marriage in this way, we should not gratefully call it a gift of God, as the preface to the new marriage service reiterates, provided that as Christians we do not try to be possessive about this gift. Nor must we imagine God as first making human beings and then giving them marriage as a present, all complete and so to speak gift-wrapped. Rather we should think

13

of marriage in any society as a way of life arising out of human nature as God made it, according to His purposes. In that sense marriage can be called a gift of God.

All this argument risks begging the question, especially if it seems to imply that there is one thing called 'marriage', the same for all peoples. What needs to be said now is that the very diversity of marriage is part of the point. Even if one leaves polygamy out of account, monogamy is not monochrome; yet in all the variety of forms the pairbond has taken in human life, there is some sense in speaking not only of pairs but also of bonds. The union between a man and a woman seems to have a built-in tendency to aspire to permanence.

Does 'aspire' give the game away? We all know that aspirations are frequently unfulfilled. Is this where ideals have to come in after all? No doubt human beings are pairing animals. There are pairbonds. But to expect them to be invariably faithful and unbreakable is surely quite another matter? Is it the permanence not the pairing, which is ideal and maybe attainable by only a few?

There is an agreeable little anecdote in Konrad Lorenz's book *On Aggression*:

I was working with Helga Fisher through her goose records and . . . I evidently showed disappointment that Heinroth's type of perfect goose marriage, faithful unto death, was so rarely to be found among our many geese. Whereupon Helga, exasperated by my disappointment, made the immortal remark, 'What do you expect? After all, geese are only human!'[16]

We know too well that human beings are only human. But far from this being the moment to abandon the notion of faithful monogamous marriage as a norm for human beings, this is just where the notion of a norm comes into its own. A norm is not a law without exceptions, but a concept we need to understand the given facts. We cannot explain what marriage is, as we find it, without the idea, quite often attained, of permanence as its hope. Fidelity is not an external condition demanded of people who get married, a sort of price to be paid for being allowed to live together, but part of the meaning of their undertaking. Without the intention of fidelity we should not call their coming together 'getting married'. Unfaithfulness is often only too actual, but it has to be a subsidiary notion, parasitic upon faithfulness.

– 3 –

Fidelity

Christians know that marriage is 'for better for worse', but sometimes this is made to sound more like a threat than a promise. It ought to mean, 'whatever happens, we can count upon each other'. It is a travesty to make it mean 'even if we regret it we are still lumbered with each other for life'.

Robert Runcie, *One Light for One World*

PROMISING

A likely comment on all this is 'That is all very well, but . . .'. Of course the intention of fidelity is built into the situation when two young people say to each other 'I love you'; and of course if they go on to have offspring the children need the stability of a continuing relationship. But sceptical voices are asking why we try to make this into an unbreakable bond for the rest of their lives. Why do we think it suitable that people should solemnly promise to stay faithful for ever? We need an answer to the question whether the marriage vows are an example of what is nowadays called 'overkill'.

In a discussion in *Philosophy* on 'Marital faithfulness',[1] Susan Mendus set the problem by quoting from Hardy's *Jude the Obscure*:

And so . . . the two swore that at every other time in their lives, till death took them, they would assuredly believe, feel, and desire precisely as they had believed, felt, and desired during the few preceding weeks. What was as remarkable as the undertaking itself was the fact that nobody seemed at all surprised at what they swore.

Marriage vows can easily be made to seem most unwise, a sort of folly resulting from being in love. It is natural for human beings to believe that nothing will ever make them change their minds, but we all know that quite often they do. Yet we encourage them to think that they are doing something irrevocable. Indeed if we are traditionalists we do our best to make the marriage bond as unbreakable as possible, even though individuals have to pay the price. If on the other hand we go along with the current tendency to accept divorce as an allowable way out, are we consistent to keep these solemn

15

vows at all? What do we suppose that they mean? What right do we have to say every time 'It was a lovely wedding', not seeming to care about the integrity of the bridegrooms and brides offering themselves up like sacrifices at our altars? Unless we seriously believe that vows are something more than a solemn statement of present hopes, would it be more realistic and honest to change the wording of our rituals, and let people marry each other in a more provisional way? That is the problem we ought to face.

Before wedding vows can be defended, some distinctions need to be made, to sort out various ways of committing oneself for the future which are less binding than vows. Suppose I say 'I am going to London tomorrow', I am telling you what I plan to do. If you see me still in the neighbourhood, you may be surprised but you ought not to feel injured. If you had counted on my absence and my change of mind has inconvenienced you, that is bad luck.

People do make undertakings which commit them more than simple statements of intention but are still not vows. For instance they make contracts, which are not at all mysterious. We may arrange that you will pay me so much to drive you to London. Then if I fail to do it you may resort to various kinds of pressure and eventually to a court of law. But if we agree, amicably or crossly, to let the contract lapse, then it lapses. It is nobody else's business to object, and no kind of metaphysical obligation has been set up.

A promise is more solemn than a contract, though not necessarily in legal form. If I promise to drive you to London, then I undertake to do it whether I want to or not and whether or not you have any way of making me do it. There may be conditions: 'if you are ready by nine' or 'if it doesn't snow'; but not 'if I feel like it'. You have a moral right that I should keep my word if I possibly can, unless I am truly prevented or you positively let me off. But I do not have to do it enthusiastically: a promise is kept even if it is kept grim-faced.

Philosophers have found promises more puzzling than contracts, because it can seem as if saying 'I promise' brings a sort of thing into the world which nobody can get rid of once it is there even if it proves entirely inconvenient. If I promise not to tell a secret, what is this padlock on my lips which stops me later from preventing a misunderstanding with an explanation? The answer is that promising is not creating a mysterious kind of object which will rise up like a ghost that nobody can exorcize. Promising is giving my word in a particular way. As Susan Mendus explains it, promises can be broken, but what does not make sense is to make a promise and at the same time contemplate breaking it.

Mrs Micawber says that she will never desert Mr Micawber. If she were to add 'but I might change my mind', she would not be making a promise. In fact human beings generally think they do understand what they are doing when they promise, and have generally found the possibility of setting up trust between people by this means a definite convenience. Keeping promises has been an important and useful part of morality since earliest times. 'He that sweareth unto his neighbour and disappointeth him not, though it were to his own hindrance'[2] is described as fit to dwell in the tabernacle of the Lord.

But this tidying up of statements, contracts and promises brings the difficulty about marriage vows to a head. For a vow requires me not just to do this or that but to put my heart into it. The difficulties multiply when I ask what it can possibly mean to pledge not just my future actions but my future feelings. And yet, if I promise fidelity before God, how can any human being ever let me off?

The problem of lifelong vows is more than an interesting intellectual puzzlement. Sooner or later we shall have to face the practical challenge that the notion of fidelity is a contribution to human misery. As an example of this challenge we can single out an article, not new but especially sharp, by Robert Chester in the *Marriage Guidance Bulletin*.[3] 'Are you', he asks, 'really concerned to strengthen family life and promote human happiness, or are you in fact seeking to preserve a particular moral code?' His topic is 'Family and marriage in the post-parental years', and he paints a dismal picture of staleness and discontent, backing it with a quantity of sociological evidence. He arrives at the blunt question, 'Would it matter if a much higher proportion of post-parental marriages were to break up?' If the answer given is that it does matter, he goes on to ask 'to whom, in what ways, and from what point of view?'

Other sociologists and many married people would give an entirely different picture of those years when the children have grown up; but the happier one's own impressions, the less one has the right to brush aside such persistent questions on behalf of other people. It is not so obviously easy for Christians to give an adequate reply. The usual reasons break in our hands. Traditionalists have always affirmed that the purpose of marriage is to bring up children. Constructive modern thought affirms that the purpose of marriage is relationship. But in the weary marriages under consideration, neither children nor relationship are any longer present: so why should either traditionalists or liberals try doggedly to keep such marriages in being? But if we give way and stop insisting on permanence and exclusiveness we seem to belittle the commitment human beings firmly believe they have made. So we are offered, it appears, a choice between upholding an arid legalism of the marriage vow or slipping into a shallow romanticism of immediate happiness: 'You must be punished for saying what it turns out that you did not mean' or 'Why should you not just please yourselves whatever you said before?'

Joining in this discussion have been voices, not wholly irresponsible, telling us that all these troubles come from taking the whole business of sex and commitment too seriously. Upholders of the traditional morality are accused of binding heavy burdens, grievous to be borne, and laying them on other people's shoulders, without being able to offer a happiness reliable enough to be worth it. If only, the critics have suggested, we would try to be more light-hearted about it all, some people would still find the deeper satisfactions, fewer would get hurt, and many would be far happier than at present. In this sort of context, most of the arguments we try to offer for permanence can look like ways of using it as a stick to beat other people.

When the continuing argument had reached this stage, along came AIDS. It has been fatally easy for moralists, substituting threats for reasons, to suggest that AIDS really is a sort of fire and brimstone raining down from heaven upon this corrupt generation. Casual sexual relationships used to be recognized as sinfully imprudent and then had a few years of seeming, with contraception, to be quite consistent with moral responsibility. Then AIDS made them irresponsible again: until a vaccine is discovered. It is time to get off this seesaw and consider why neither a divine taboo nor 'safe sex' is the whole story.

Suppose eventually the problem of AIDS is solved medically. Will Christians be able to be thoroughly glad at this dreadful fear being lifted, or will they have little twinges of regret that one of their best arguments for chastity has been removed too? Will they eat their words and acknowledge that the 'permissive society' can take over again after all? It would be wiser to keep their heads now and commend fidelity for its own sake, not as a regrettably necessary medical precaution. The moral aspects of the AIDS crisis are more complex and subtle than any simple 'I told you so'.

In the end we neither can nor should defend our beliefs about human relationships by threats. The questions which were being pressed upon us before the arrival of AIDS are still there. How can people bind themselves for the future? To make vows seems presumptuous, and to require people to fulfil them seems cruel. The preliminary digging we have tried to do has apparently landed us in quite a deep hole. It is all very well for Christians to rely upon the helicopter of divine grace to come to rescue them. But can we really be content to leave the non-Christians in this hole where vows mean little or nothing, or to see some of them scramble out of the difficulty by simply denying the importance of vows anyway, knocking down the carefully-built structures of human constancy and trust? We have more in common with our fellow beings than that and ought not cheerfully to leave them in holes. If as Christians we believe that we are all made in God's image, we should be more aware, not less, of humanity as something belonging to us all and of the capacity for real fidelity as built into our humanity.

HUMAN CAPACITY

Fidelity is a problem not an answer. When people want to keep their vows, they do not think of themselves as keeping vows. When they do not want to, we cannot very well argue them into it. We can go on for a while talking about the importance of stability and the needs of children and the common good; but sometimes it will begin to seem that we are putting a mere legal form before people and that for everyone's good, including even the children's, leniency is the best policy. But then honesty persists in asking, what was the point of making people promise lifelong fidelity, if when things get difficult they can be let off?

If one believes that the human institution of marriage, not just as an ideal, but as a common reality, is a great good, then for that very reason it must be able to maintain itself in its own right and not be paid for in the currency of other people's misery. We are only too well aware that we are confronted by unhappy people, unhappy in different ways for lack of fidelity. To tell them that fidelity is the solution to their trouble is as unhelpful as saying that food is the answer to a famine. Nor shall we be allowed to forget the complaint that some people are, so to say, over-fed with fidelity and could do with less of it.

Some too easy ways of looking for an answer ought to be ruled out. In particular, fidelity cannot be applied as a kind of cement to mend holes in human relationships. We need to understand what it means better than that before we can make it work for us. It is wrong to say 'when love has gone, fidelity can hold a relationship together'. It is really no better to say, as is frequently said to young couples, 'You will find that romance will fade but fidelity will grow to fill the gap'.

Fidelity makes no sense as a substitute for something else which is presumed to be missing. It is the stuff of a good relationship. It is quite defeatist to look on fidelity as a crutch for an ailing marriage or as a patch on an old worn-out one. What we are asking is what this stuff is and how it may reliably be made.

To see fidelity in action we need to look at marriage in good shape rather than marriage in trouble. What fidelity does is make viaducts across the uneven landscapes of life. That is what 'for better, for worse' ought to mean. But when marriage falters, to call for fidelity is only to put a name to the problem. When it has faltered and failed, to expect fidelity to remain like a grin without a cat is to make it into a sort of unknown quantity like an x in algebra.

Just because marriage is distinctive among relationships and characterized by its one-to-one exclusiveness, there is no need to imagine that it must have belonging to it a distinct kind of faithfulness concentrating entirely upon 'forsaking all other'. When the exclusiveness has to be brought right into the foreground like that, and the main point of marriage seems to be not having affairs with other people, something has already gone wrong. It is no wonder that to make vows of fidelity becomes puzzling, either unnecessary or unreasonable.

It is time to look at what fidelity is rather than what it is not, and in particular to set marital fidelity in its context in human life, rather than treating it as a mysterious way of keeping marriages in being, which does not usually come into play until too late to be any good. The ordinary faithfulness of marriage is a special instance of a capacity human beings characteristically have to be constant to each other in small matters and large, to keep their pledged word and maintain their affections. Fidelity in this sense is not an unknown x. It is the foundation of the human tendency to build relationships of many kinds. We can hardly get on without it, though we have to make allowance for lapses. It would not be overstating the case to say that it is the bonds between us that make us fully human. Because we have this capacity we can develop all the relationships we know, friendship, pairbond, parenthood, into continuing forms of love: not exactly unique to our species, but characteristic of it.

To say this is to lay the foundation for a way of understanding human life which may, with care, be called 'personalism'. We first describe people as 'relationship-forming beings' and then we fit particular relationships, such as marriage, into the picture. Fidelity is not a sort of extra obligation some people take on, wisely or unwisely, but part of the structure of our interdependence, expressing itself in many ways.

The insights personalism can yield about what fidelity means in marriage could be lost by rushing at it. We could take a quick short cut and say that fidelity is simply love, the love that makes the world go round. We are made for love and love is what we all need: but to say that is not particularly illuminating. Love also can be a problem not an answer. The greatest Christian poet took a whole Divine Comedy to reach it. If 'love' unexplained is brought into the discussion too early it can be just an argument-stopper, a way of losing sight of the variety of human relationships.

'Fidelity' keeps in mind a more complex picture, including the faithfulness of the martyr who must serve God rather than men, the impersonal integrity of the manufacturer who will not fob off shoddy goods on to the public, the accuracy of the scholar for whom truth does not wobble, the solidarity of the trade unionist with fellow workers, or the trained obedience of the soldier doing an unpleasant duty. Any of these can go bad. Human nature being what it is, we have bigots, prigs, pedants and plain brutes. Married fidelity can go bad too. There are shrewish wives and battered wives, husbands who dominate or are dominated, tyrants and victims, proud of their faithfulness. The corruption of the best is the worst. It is what we most need and cannot jettison that has to run the risk of going bad; so it is still in order to look at the best and not only reckon with the worst.

A central meaning of the fidelity we need is integrity, not only within oneself but towards other people. Fidelity is a matter of wholeness; of, as it were, moving in one piece. I am not to say one thing and do another, or keep up a pleasing public façade which my private conduct belies. My 'image' is to be the real 'me'. Immediately we must go on to say that the kind of fidelity in relationships which we are trying to track down must be something more, something, so to say, warmer. The maintenance of integrity is not enough. Integrity is too cool and even too self-regarding to be the whole meaning of fidelity. There must be an element of what religious people call 'self-giving'. The problem is to put in this warmth without melting all our concepts together into vague and unhelpful platitudes.

Self-giving is too easily used as a moralizing way of talking about love; and once again, moving to 'love' too quickly can be to take a hasty short cut. To capture the notion of fidelity, we need to keep love and integrity both in focus at once. We have a notion less inward-looking than 'integrity', more able to take other people into account: the concept of honesty, so obviously important in human life as to be readily overlooked. Of course the giving of oneself is a matter of love; but also, and just as much to the present purpose, it is a matter of truth. Fidelity in human relationships has everything to do with giving to somebody else what one really is. A handy though hackneyed metaphor is the idea of openness. A faithful person is open as the day, straightforward not devious.

TRANSPARENCY

A less overworked metaphor is 'transparency'. Whereas openness emphasizes lack of defence and vulnerability, transparency emphasizes clarity and lack of concealment. It is direct and simple enough to bring the idea of fidelity down from lofty heights to a level where something quite practical can be said about what truth in relationship needs to be.

To be faithful is traditionally to be 'true'. It is obvious, but not too obvious to need pointing out, that truth really does have something definite to do with truthfulness. The metaphor of faithful people as transparent to one another helps to restore this easily-lost emphasis. No doubt fidelity means much more than truthfulness; but unless fidelity has its roots in truthfulness, indeed in the simple notion of truth-telling, we shall find that it has no proper foothold in the real world. To spell out what this means could be a way of making the idea of fidelity less problematic.

John Austin Baker, now Bishop of Salisbury, in *The Foolishness of God*, has refreshingly set out to rehabilitate the virtue of thoroughgoing truthfulness as 'an ardent and exhilarating virtue', urging that if we would stop depending 'on the comforts of evasion, half-truth, flattery, and the double-talk of official statements', we should find that 'a climate of truth would not necessarily be one of keen winds and cold seas only'. He grants that there are 'well-known classic exceptions' to the absolute duty of truth-telling, but insists that many of the difficulties arise 'because people are accustomed to lies and require them'.[4]

Many people would half agree with him; but still it is usual to operate with the idea that although big lies are sins, little lies, white lies, are not only excusable but acceptable, certainly not contrary to the possession of an important virtue like fidelity: 'I had a lovely time'; 'I have a bit of a headache'. What is wrong with saying easy things like this to smooth out difficulties? It goes against the grain of common-sense morality to suggest that little lies could be even more damaging to the fabric of human trust than big ones. They are more insidious because we do not take them seriously. The necessary triviality of any example of a small lie makes it sound fussy to point out that when people stop thinking of truth-telling as important, communication with them gradually becomes impossible: 'Does she mean it or is she just saying the first thing that comes into her head?' The transparency of human relationships is clouded just as much by a foggy atmosphere of acceptable white lies as by the solid obstruction of the great black lie. To lie to people is to conceal reality from them.

Sometimes we are aware that people are setting up barriers of their own, and these we ought to respect. We can hardly blame them if they lie to us, if in our aggressive demands upon them we break through shields and disperse smokescreens which have been put there on purpose. Faithfulness and sincerity do not mean that everyone must always be fully transparent to everyone else. But when can self-protection justify barricading oneself behind deceit? Instead of always assuming that lies are to be judged by size, the smaller the better, we can recognize that lying is a kind of weaponry, and ask what justifies its use. What counts is the validity of the reason, not the size of the lie.

The murderer chasing his intended victim is to be lied to, not directed. That is one of the 'well-known classic exceptions'. The badgering reporter is less dramatic and more human, but can in a similar way forfeit his right to be told the truth. Jane Austen's Elinor confronted with a foolish young man at a party 'agreed to it all, for she did not think he deserved the compliment of rational opposition'.[5] In other words, he had squandered his claim upon her transparency.

Ordinarily the claim to be told the truth ought to stand, whether for trivial matters or great. A friend choosing a new frock, a would-be author with a manuscript, a patient asking for a diagnosis: to tell any of these what they want to hear whether it is true or not is to hide reality from them, to spoil the times when the truth is also welcome, and to cloud not to clear our relationship with them.

Of course people would rather not be told that colours do not suit them, and still less that their books are no good or that they are mortally ill. But they would still rather be able to believe good news when it happens to be true, without always thinking 'but that is what she would have said anyway'.

It ought not to be surprising that fidelity is an exacting virtue, needing courage on both sides. There is often no evident way to steer between woolly kindness and blunt harshness. There will be plenty of times when we shall not know what we ought to say and do. Ought I to make a dying relative miserable by refusing to give a promise which looks intolerable to keep? If I have made such a promise and now think I was wrong, is it binding however unhappy the upshot will be for the living? This truly is a hard case. Our intuitions have some weight but are not infallible. The account of fidelity as transparency in relationship allows the hard cases to be as hard as they are without forcing our intuitions into a straitjacket.

Does any of this help in understanding the fidelity of the pairbond? When two people take each other as husband and wife, forsaking all other, the most coherent foundation for this ambitious undertaking is a sharing of two lives based on transparent truthfulness. It seems typical of human beings to want this kind of commitment enough to make it worth the stresses it is capable of generating. People are, characteristically though not automatically, prepared to make great sacrifices in its name. When the sacrifices are particularly great we talk in admiration about heroic fidelity. But what the marriage vows directly undertake is not heroism but the kind of everyday trustworthiness which is there 'through thick and thin'. That is something about which it makes good sense to make promises. To bring into the foreground in this way the comprehensible requirement of transparency is not to play down the special exclusiveness of marriage but to give it a practical basis. What matters is that fidelity belongs to a relationship in being, and does not merely linger to haunt it after a disaster.

A good illustration of the interplay between ordinary and special faithfulness is the tragedy of Othello and Desdemona. Desdemona is, in a most ordinary sense, a faithful wife, an 'innocent party'. She is chaste and she loves her husband; but it is shallow simply to take her part and to see the play as the pathetic story of a woman's fidelity and a man's jealousy. It is more deeply tragic as a play about a culturally mixed marriage, with elements of promise and incomprehension woven closely into it from the start. The disastrous outcome is not because Othello and Desdemona are black and white, but because Othello is not able to refute Iago's allegation that the Venetian ladies do not take fidelity very seriously. But that is still not the whole story. These lovers are not 'star-crossed'. The collapse of their union is not entirely a matter of misunderstanding. Unlike Cordelia, who starts with the rather unlovable integrity of being truthful on principle, Desdemona is not profoundly honest: 'She did deceive her father'. It is when Othello is reminded of this that he is not able to go on saying 'My life upon her faith'.[6] So their friendship, not their love, is destroyed; and fidelity is defeated. The proper comprehensive faithfulness of their marriage never develops.

Desdemona's penultimate words are a noble lie, that she has killed herself. Her last words are, if one considers, equally untruthful: 'Commend me to my kind lord'. They are the sort of instinctive untruth, like her lie about the handkerchief, which tries to blunt the edge of a reality which cannot be faced. Othello repudiates it instantly: 'She's like a liar gone to burning hell; 'Twas I that killed her'. In his hideous error he has grasped something real. He is not simply a jealous husband. His lack of faith is unjust but not arbitrary: it is grounded in her lack of transparency, which gave Iago's lies about her matrimonial fidelity the chance to take hold. The poignancy of the tragedy is that we have been given plenty of glimpses along the way of what this union could have been like.

MOMENTUM

Of course truthfulness is not the whole of matrimonial fidelity. Faithfulness in marriage is something over and above being true and just in all one's dealings: it is committing oneself to another person for the whole of the future. What we have done so far is fill in part of the substance of this commitment so as to make it less mysterious and to keep it related to the other commitments of our lives. But we have hardly begun to explain how commitment can bind people for the future. How can it be possible by making a vow to pledge oneself for ever, or even for long? What does a promise add to the world? Must we imagine it as a kind of action done now which somehow takes away one's freedom to do other actions in the future?

We need another metaphor. A hopeful picture of what happens when people make promises is the idea of gathering momentum. Human life is not one separate act after another, each a fresh start, any more than human beings are fundamentally separate entities independent of their relationship to each other. Ronald Knox is supposed to have said, horribly but humanly: 'A man's first duty is to his plans'. We constantly limit our own freedom, not by mysterious metaphysical liabilities but by the momentum our lives will gather. We are self-propelling, and in that sense are free agents; but the ground is not flat and we are seldom stationary.

To promise, we may say, is deliberately to plunge in a particular direction. It is not just chance that we are still heading in that direction when we come to keep the promise. Life, and especially our interrelationship with other people, will have a sufficient tendency to carry us there that it is not irresponsible to expect to arrive. To make vows for life is more like starting downhill on a bicycle than making an announcement about our future intentions. The surprise is when people stop, not when they carry on. What we do about the damage to themselves and other people when they stop too suddenly; how we help them to gain fresh momentum when they come to a slow halt: these are practical problems. But practical problems do not make it nonsense to embark upon enterprises which will take hold of us in ways which we cannot fully predict. It will be easier to be of use to those who fall by the way if we are not trying to pretend that they do not exist or to punish them for spoiling a theory.

The philosopher J. L. Austin illuminated the idea of a promise by explaining that to say 'I promise' is not to make a peculiar sort of statement about our present state of mind which in some extraordinary way binds us to go on like that for ever. A promise, he insisted, is not really a kind of statement at all but a kind of action.[7] We do something by saying something. He used the very example of

25

marriage. By making vows, people actually marry each other, not just say what is going through their minds. To marry, a Christian can thoroughly agree, is to take each other as husband and wife before witnesses. It is to make a plunge, not a prediction. It may be a daring plunge, like Macaulay's Horatius leaping into the Tiber and pausing as he went, not in hesitation but for blessing:

> A Roman's life, a Roman's arms,
> Take thou in charge this day.

To make a vow is not as it were to summon out of nothingness a sort of *thing* called a marriage bond, which is then mysteriously indestructible, but to move decisively forward in a way which is expressly designed not to keep options open. A vow is not an invisible magic spell, though like any definite action it has effects in the real world which are liable to be irrevocable, and which in this case are meant to be irrevocable.

The idea of momentum can be explained less impersonally with the help of a very different philosopher, Gabriel Marcel, who puzzled a great deal about what promises could be. Vows are not just plunges, but plunges into relationships: 'There is no commitment', he insisted, 'purely from my own side. . . . All commitment is a response'.[8] Other people are not passive. They exert a pull on us. The momentum to which we entrust ourselves is not a whirlpool of impersonal forces but a sort of dance, in which we may have to learn the steps as we go along, but not in isolation. Fidelity, we may say, is the constant pattern which emerges from all this, naturally but not effortlessly, as a result of the commitment, formal or informal, of joining in.

− 4 −
Exclusiveness

I would there were no age between sixteen and three-and-twenty, or that youth would sleep out the rest; for there is nothing in the between but getting wenches with child, wronging the ancientry, stealing, fighting.

William Shakespeare, *The Winter's Tale* III:3

PROMISE BROKEN

What is the permanent effect of a vow? Suppose after all it is broken, what remains? How can we say both that it must never be broken and that sometimes it can be? Looking forward, we say 'Never'; looking back, we hardly know what to say. Are these people who have failed in their undertakings to be treated as traitors: whether because that is what we really believe they are, or simply *'pour encourager les autres'*? What to do about a broken vow is a recalcitrant example of the old problem of punishment and deterrence. One may have no particular wish to exact the advertised penalty and may even feel that it will only make matters worse, but as the point of the penalty was to deter other people from presumption, so to waive the penalty must tend to give permission for future presumption.

What remains when a vow is broken must be the right it conferred to refuse another chance. The simplest way to treat broken vows seriously is to say firmly 'Never again': but there are several different things that 'Never again' can mean. It may say simply: 'I am too angry to forgive you or ever to trust you again. You have had your chance and lost it. Your broken vows will hang around your neck for evermore.' That is an entirely valid response, for which people who make solemn undertakings and then break them must be prepared. A main meaning of a vow is that it incurs this liability. There can be no claim upon a second chance. The difficulty is that among kind-hearted people, let alone among professed Christians, we simply cannot give up hope of forgiveness. If we love mercy, it is a natural inclination to say 'Never mind' instead of 'Never again'; at the risk of letting vows become meaningless.

So does 'Never again' mean 'I should like to give you a second chance but I must not'? This version of rigorism, which is practical rather than theoretical, has a good deal to be said for it. The experienced consequences of easy second chances, it has to be admitted, do put a large question mark against the liberalism one would dearly like to maintain. People soon stop being amazed at being shown undeserved kindness, and begin to expect it and even count upon it. So must forgiveness, however tempting, be forbidden for the sake of everyone else? To show mercy to people who are in full view has another face which may look very like injustice to people who are out of sight. It is bitterly hard for the children of a first marriage, 'innocent parties' *par excellence*, to see a father or mother merrily remarried in church or elaborately blessed, with a new partner who may even be partly responsible for the undoing of the union now put asunder. The injustice to young people who are getting married for the first time, deprived of the firm assurance that the vows they want to make really mean something, is less obvious but possibly more pervasive. Kindness to penitent sinners is difficult to distinguish practically from advance encouragement to the unscrupulous.

The present confusion in the Church of England about the remarriage of divorced people is deeply damaging, because false messages, incompatible but strong, are coming through from both liberalism and rigorism. Liberals seem to say that divorce does not matter, rigorists that divorce is all that matters. Those who believe that the rigorist false message is the more misleading, and that for Christians mercy must somehow be allowed to prevail, have a particularly large obligation to all concerned to make it plain that mercy is not a matter of course but a special dispensation. It is not fair to anyone to let vows simply vanish. If the Church of England is ever to implement its now long-standing resolution[1] that in suitable circumstances divorced people might be allowed to remarry in church, what is needed is not a rule for the breaking of rules, not 'guidelines' to state in advance who is to be eligible for mercy, but a way of openly releasing people from their past while making it clear what we are doing. Mercy, as well as justice, needs to be 'seen to be done'. Liberals must find some responsible alternative to the 'never again' of rigorism, an authorized new beginning which will at least include the acknowledgement that more people than the two who are now in love with one another have their happiness at stake.

Not surprisingly, Christians who are not rigorists or liberals are often convinced that these arguments about forgiveness are missing the point. 'Never again' may not be a matter of 'We refuse to forgive you' or even of 'It is bad policy to forgive you', but rather, 'We do forgive you but forgiveness cannot undo the past'. It is a conviction about vows which to many people seems the obvious reason for refusing a church wedding after a divorce, even to people who do not hold a rigorist view of Christ's teaching. Is it not common sense that once vows are broken it is simply impossible to make new ones? So it seems that the register office is the place for a new union and maybe the Church can bless it, but a second church wedding is simply ruled out.[2]

This conviction does justice to the difficulty of making a fresh start but is not entirely logical after all. Common sense knows quite well that sometimes people can be let off from keeping promises. The notion of dispensation, even from religious vows, is not nonsense. Whether we like it or not, to make a vow is not to look backwards to the past but forwards to a still unknown future. If a marriage, or a remarriage, is made by a man and a woman solemnly taking one another as husband and wife before witnesses, they are in effect making vows, even if old broken vows lie behind their present hopes. Rigorists could logically say that what they are doing is altogether invalid, that the first marriage stands; pessimists may say that they ought not to be encouraged; but what does not make sense is to say that their remarriage may be acknowledged but not with vows. The case for remarriage in church, with clear new promises, rests upon honesty, not weakness. Putting asunder does happen and it certainly looks as if real new unions do happen and are sometimes the best outcome; so although the past cannot be undone we may sometimes hope to put it behind us. A fresh start, if people can have one at all, is not best made in a half-hearted way.

People want formal fresh starts because they mind about fidelity and know that it is not merely an unattainable ideal. A remarriage aspires to be a marriage. The notion of remarriage after divorce depends upon the positive idea of lasting marriage as a reality within our ordinary experience. If people who have made vows and broken them can find someone to trust them for the future after all, their enterprise may be dangerous, it may be disloyal in ways we must hesitate to countenance; but it is not essentially illogical. If the Church is to bless their undertaking it must make up its mind whether this is likely to be God's will; it must act as a Church, taking the responsibility to bind and loose; and it must make it clear to all concerned what is going on. Piecemeal kindness is bound to give the impression that fidelity does not matter any more.

LIMITS?

To the question 'What does fidelity mean, as a going concern?' two answers have seemed promising. The first is that here and now fidelity is a matter of transparency, of not surrounding other people with fog. The second answer is that to ask about the future 'How can I be faithful?' has really no answer, if the emphasis is solely on the 'I'. I could not undertake, all on my own, to be faithful for ever. A marriage vow is not a promise I make to myself. What I can do is undertake with energy and goodwill to allow someone else to elicit from me the faithfulness we want and need. Fidelity develops as an unselfconscious virtue: something that happens to us rather than something we do. The most we can do is be ready to receive and give it.

This is simply the Christian doctrine of justification by faith rather than by works, of grace rather than merit, given application to human life as well as to religion. People who are fortunate enough to believe in God will add divine grace into the picture: we are not wholly dependent upon one another and His faithfulness will eventually be able to elicit ours in full.

People who are fortunate enough to believe in God have a besetting tendency to let the argument run away with them, to assume what they have not yet shown. Critics are suggesting that all the problems about the permanence of vows and the possibility or impossibility of remarrying come from expecting too much. Of course fidelity is an admirable ideal, but it still needs to be made plain why after all it has to last for ever and ever. Could it never be worthwhile for it just to go on for a good long time? Is it naïve to put such moral weight on the pairbond, when the idea really belongs in quite a down-to-earth way to the story of our evolution as human beings? Fidelity between parents is useful for the protection of human young during their long childhood. By what right, we need to know, have its demands been extended to cover people's whole lives until death parts them?

We still need an answer to the argument that the pairbond might conveniently be allowed to revert to its biological purpose, so that we would treat marriage as an alliance for bringing up a family. Childless people and parents of grown-up children could make what long- or short-term arrangements they saw fit. Changing partners would seem more like moving house and less like unfaithfulness than we have always believed. Has birth control made this ethic a live option? The wages of sin down the ages have been unwanted progeny. Now that babies can be avoided, many people will take a great deal of persuading that the sin is still sin.

Can morality change? It is no wonder that traditionalists are aghast at such an idea. It seems that our tradition is being abandoned and that our contemporaries are being left with only one remaining rule, 'Never have an unwanted baby'. Maybe neither traditionalists nor radicals in this argument are taking contraception seriously enough.

Traditionalists are forgetting that when the facts change our very same morality may need to be applied in new ways. Contraception is changing the facts of human life. The notorious argument among Christians about the rights and wrongs of the choice married people now have, to plan or postpone their families, may have distracted attention from the possible moral relevance of the choice unmarried lovers now have to leave babies out of account. A main prop of the traditional argument against unconventional liaisons has been knocked away. The most obvious irresponsibility of cohabitation outside marriage seems to have evaporated: does this, or does it not, make some difference to our understanding of God's will for unmarried people? The question has to be reopened.

Radicals on the other hand who look on traditional morality as a long-established tyranny have forgotten how new, for the human race, is this ability to separate human pairing from inescapable procreation. For all the centuries until now babies have been unpredictable, or rather, only too predictable. Traditional prohibitions on unregulated sexuality were not inexplicable taboos but the only way to keep the rule, of which all concerned can see the point, that children are not to be irresponsibly brought into the world. Once this rule did require the keeping of three other rules: No sex outside marriage; No marriage unless you can support a family; and, Look after women so that they can be secure in their motherhood. Now each of these rules has lost part of its point and this does make a difference. 'Thou shalt not' has lost its obvious relevance. To ask where we stand now is not necessarily to sell the pass.

Unfortunately Christian moralists have let themselves get on the defensive. Some garbled and superficial lessons from Freud have confused the issue. From fear of uncontrolled sexuality we should have moved on towards appreciation of the whole person, body and spirit together: but often the move has been towards a new fear, of any attempt to control sexuality. Because we have come to realize that the physical nature of human beings is profoundly sexual, it has come to be an accepted orthodoxy that all relationship is sexual relationship, to the extent that it is almost a human right to express even slight forms of commitment in a fully physical way. Once we accept the thorough goodness of our bodily natures we find ourselves repeatedly faced with the question why some particular relationship

31

should 'stop short' of its fullest physical expression. Any resistance to such tolerance is heard as an attempt to revert to an unacceptable and prudish dualism, exalting spirit over body.

It needs to be made more clear by Christian moralists that a permissive sexual ethic ought to be criticized for not doing justice to the rich variety of human relationships. There are many ways in which human beings relate to one another, and to suggest that the end of them all should have to be the same is limiting, not liberating. Integrity in relationship is a matter of keeping commitment and its expression in step. What is wrong with the sin called 'fornication' is not that something unauthorized is being *done*, which might be punished by a baby or an illness, but on the contrary that something deeply belonging to our human nature is *lacking*. In sexual union which does not aspire to permanence, the commitment of a man and a woman to one another is being both given and withheld.

Promiscuity is not at the centre of the argument. Although radical moralists set about defending it, before AIDS arrived, as the healthiest form of sport, traditionalists have no need to feel defenceless or even outnumbered. Moral criticism is neither prudish nor outdated in objecting to sexual activity being regarded as entirely physical with no moral and emotional bond. When sex means no more than bodily pleasure, without being a sign of any real human relationship, then assuredly something has gone wrong; though moralists will need to be sensitive in deciding what. What are people looking for when they become promiscuous? They may be coolly pleasing themselves or frantically seeking for something lacking in their lives. In trying to keep options open they may shut off the satisfying option of lifelong stability. If ever sin is to be called 'missing the mark', promiscuity is a good example.

The harder moral argument is about relationships which are physical, emotional, social and even high-minded, but decline to be irrevocable. Once it is granted that sexuality is not as such unclean, why must it be confined so rigidly to matrimony? Why talk about 'fornication' at all, except perhaps for relationships which are irresponsibly ephemeral? Of course faithfulness is a good and life-enhancing thing, but must it be the only consideration? To answer these questions satisfactorily in a still traditional way one must keep one's head and consider the real good and the real harm in the partial commitments.

Sometimes what is missing is fairly clear: the relationship is simply one-sided and means more to one partner than to the other. Then we do well to wonder, though not triumphantly, whether somebody is being exploited or is presently going to be hurt. It is not moralistic to be convinced that such liberty to be unshackled does not constitute a moral breakthrough.

Nor is it moralistic still to look rather suspiciously for lop-sidedness when the claim is made that options are being kept open: 'It would be nice if it lasted but if we get tired of one another it is nobody else's business. So long as we are not irresponsible or ineffi-cient enough to have a child, there is no question of blame or "immorality" if we live together for a while and then split up. Much better that than all the miserable struggle of divorce. We can try it out without getting too involved and see how we get on.' There is not much safeguard here for the emotionally weaker party against misery and bitterness not easily distinguishable from the misery and bitterness of divorce. To ask them how sure they really can be that they are totally at one in the degree of commitment is like asking a polygamist whether he can be quite sure of loving his wives equally. Practical experience is not altogether on their side.

Lovers sometimes part 'good friends'. They sometimes do after a broken marriage. But an advance promise of mature detachment is no more likely to be easy to keep in the end than an advance promise of faithfulness. How many people truly like it when their partners take care to keep their options open? This is the sort of freedom that is not so happy in the claiming as in the propounding. How many middle-aged women would want to allow the lovers of their youth to feel quite free to leave them, with no ill-feelings? Indeed how many fairly young women will go on being content with the condition they thought they could accept: no child?

Traditionalists who have taken the old morality for granted and lived contentedly by it all their lives torment themselves nowadays with the idea that this generation, maybe their own sons and daughters, are badly brought up and indeed immoral. They would be justified in forgetting the word 'fornication' but remembering these real questions about human happiness.

It is only fair to add, and even insist, that sometimes when people live together unmarried the commitment really is there, or is beginning to be there, and all that is lacking is the wedding ceremony. Instead of bandying about the idea of 'living in sin' a Christian would do well to consider honestly whether what we have here truly is a kind of marriage.

The standard way to make a marriage is a wedding. The couple take each other as husband and wife before witnesses. It is their consent that makes the marriage, not the ministrations of registrar or even priest. The wedding ceremony is a solemn way of making that consent public, and to ask for the blessing of family and friends and especially, for religious people, the blessing of God. But if what makes the marriage is consent, to dispense with the ceremony may not invalidate the consent.

There are a good many couples today who have seen the previous generation's notions about marriage and their ensuing ups and downs as hindrance rather than help. When people try to work out a different and more humanly satisfying way for themselves, it must be recognized that what they are engaged upon is a moral enterprise. At least in all seriousness let it not be nipped in the bud for the sake of respectability.

If we think, as well we may, that people who avoid formal commitment are living dangerously, we ought not to wash our hands of them but stand by to help pick up the pieces if necessary, which does not mean being ready to say 'I told you so'. We might rather say something like Wordsworth in his 'Ode to Duty':

> There are who ask not if thine eye
> Be on them; who, in love and truth,
> Where no misgiving is, rely
> Upon the genial sense of youth:
> Oh, if through confidence misplaced
> They fail, thy saving arms, dread Power! around them cast.

And when, as happens now quite often, people eventually come along from the same address asking for a church wedding after all, it is more suitable to kill the fatted calf for them than to lecture them and freeze them out. What if they are only responding to parental pressure? The Prodigal Son was responding to the pangs of hunger. To be possessive about our tradition is a most unlovely manifestation of virtue.

PROMISE KEPT

Having shown some sympathy for our contemporaries who are trying honestly to work out for themselves a home-made morality, we are at length in a position to be fair to the morality we have inherited. There is no need to be defeatist on the one hand, or heavy-handed on the other, about what marriage can be.

Defeatism indeed is partly caused by heavy-handedness. When people are given the impression that marriage is deathly serious, that the marriage bond is a chain and that only the uncommitted can have fun and enjoy themselves, it is no wonder that they begin to think worse of commitment.

The message of the radicals is that we should stop moralizing and be happy hedonists; but the message misses the point. There is a good corrective in a small book by Father Andrew Greeley called

Love and Play.[3] He simply stands the hedonist argument on its head. Far from re-emphasizing the gravity of sex, he insists that it is meant to be fun: but who are the best people to play with? Will children play with strangers? It is brief meetings that are characteristically formal. To be really light-hearted and even frivolous with somebody else takes time and trust.

What the marriage vow does at its best is not give people cause to moralize, but on the contrary, room to stop moralizing. It gives them a chance to take their relationship for granted: not indeed to presume upon it, but to let their love for each other grow without continually pulling it up by the roots to see how it is getting on. By making vows, people give their consent to belong to each other and to work out together from then on what that means for them.

Emphasis upon consent as the essence of marriage can be misunderstood. It has sometimes trapped Western Christians into legalism and a concentration on 'marital rights'. One can see why such a liberal-minded critic as D. S. Bailey, looking at the history of the Church, has even deplored 'consent' for displacing the 'one-flesh' union of husband and wife from its proper central position.[4] The value of this emphasis is quite otherwise: to safeguard the true meaning of marriage, the joining of two lives in one. There should be no need to contrast consent and consummation. Properly understood, consent looks forward to the married life it inaugurates, in its full physical and personal reality.

Far from legalistically ignoring love, free mutual consent presupposes it. To hand the rest of one's life over to somebody else makes no sense without at least the beginnings of love. When marriage has been a kind of slavery then it is fair to say that it is some kind of duress, physical or emotional, rather than consent which has joined these lives. To root the marriage union in consent is to make room for the idea that marriage is something chosen and wanted by human beings.

The point of the pairbond, of its being 'bond' as well as 'pair', is time. Biologically it fulfils the function of giving the new generation of human beings time to mature slowly under adult care; but in the providence of God, as Christians believe, human mating arrangements have taken on profound and satisfying significance for the adults themselves. It makes realistic sense to announce that marriage 'was ordained for the mutual society, help, and comfort, that the one ought to have of the other, both in prosperity and adversity'. What marriage provides above all is a stable framework on which to base a life.[5] Married people are to join their lives for as long as they both shall live in such a way as to have no remainder of the same sort for anybody else. Here alone among human relationships a certain

35

possessiveness is in place, a consciousness of mutual belonging, in which honouring involves making claims not leaving free. Something of this awareness of being claimed as a person is experienced in parenthood, but with two big differences: the relationship of parent and child is asymmetrical, and as a total demand it is temporary. Only in marriage is the claim reciprocal, exclusive and developing.

A relationship between two people is not a success or a failure once and for all, but thriving or wilting, deep-rooted or shallow. A good cohabitation could flourish more than a bad marriage; but by the time one had the right to call a cohabitation successful it would have shown the qualities to which marriage aspires, the life-enhancing reciprocity in which a man and a woman take each other to love and to cherish. There is no grim necessity for moralists to impugn the validity of such a union when it has become happily established, just because it has not been 'solemnized'.

When a couple get married, what they consent to is to be each other's lifelong companions, not to change a light-hearted relationship into a serious one. What they are to give each other above all is their time and attention, and they will develop their own style with their own light and shade, which will suit them even if it suits nobody else. It would be a shame if their wedding day turned out to be the happiest day of their lives. Robert Browning's 'Grow old along with me! The best is yet to be', if not too hastily written off as platitudinous, could be a good corrective to the sort of defeatist wedding sermon which informs the young couple that romance will fade, and promises them staid 'compensations' to fill its place.

Even romance is not bound to fade away, though it is fair enough to say that nobody could base a whole life upon a sole diet of it. The potential happiness of middle age and old age is not a consolation prize for the absence of romance but an authentic development from what romance has promised. To insist upon the right to change partners in youth may be to undermine the hope of this way of flourishing in due time.[6] So an immensely valuable form of human happiness could go by default, the fundamental trust which can develop when marriage is fully monogamous. This possibility of happiness is worth protection lest it should disappear before it is even missed.

To hold out this realistically solid hope is not to forget the troubles of life: on the contrary. When trouble comes, illness, disappointment, bereavements, unemployment, difficulty in making ends meet, strains and shocks of all kinds: that is when the marriage vows come into their own. The world is a frightening and often uncomfortable place, but one has somebody in it who can be counted on 'for better, for worse, for richer, for poorer, in sickness and in health'; who has not said only 'Let's see if it works out'. It is no wonder that people marry again even after a divorce: there is something in this notion of belonging to one another that they deeply want.

– 5 –

Christian teaching

It is the curse of 'Christian morality' that it always regards the most legalistic view as the 'most serious'.

Emil Brunner, *The Divine Imperative*

BACK TO THE BIBLE?

Suppose that marriage is a kind of norm in human life. Suppose that fidelity is within reach. What has become of the distinctiveness and difficulty of the Christian way, which believers have tried to follow and sceptics have rejected as too hard for human nature? Is discipleship really quite easy, with no question of taking up a cross? Attempts to make our teaching suit everyone can look soft and even disloyal in the light of the Gospel, where notoriously there are some 'hard sayings'. At least we ought to be clear about which way we are going.

The idea that marriage is meant to make people happy is, of course, thoroughly Christian: so long as it does. But when people are not so happy, is that the time to press on with trying to please them, or to urge them to take up their cross? The trouble with the gentle alternative is that it can seem to make the Gospel irrelevant. The trouble with the stern alternative is that it becomes a way of binding heavy burdens, grievous to be borne, upon *other* people's shoulders.

A look back over only about the last thirty years or so shows a marked change in the presuppositions of Christian people. As recently as the 1960s the conviction was taken really seriously that anyone who divorced his wife and married another was literally 'living in sin' and could hardly be allowed even to receive Communion, let alone be married again in church. Now Christians are not ashamed of positively hoping that a divorced spouse will soon find happiness again with somebody else. Humanly speaking, we have left behind a good deal of unlovely legalism. But have we also got out of the habit of taking to heart the teaching of the Lord? What in fact are we doing about what we find in the New Testament?

This is not a clear-cut problem of a shift or slide into permissiveness and what to do about it. The understanding of the Bible, and therefore of the Lord's teaching, has itself become a kind of battleground: or rather, radicals and fundamentalists have drawn apart into opposing camps which are not quite sure of each other's whereabouts. The scholarly study of the books of both the Old and the New Testaments has become so technical that the Book that the Reformers placed in all our hands seems to have been taken away again.

If one tries to be a Christian moralist or some sort of lay theologian, one can neither evade the use of the Bible nor dare to dogmatize about it. One is conscious all the time of hungry sheep on the one hand, and of learned and keen-minded critics breathing down one's neck on the other. Understandably there is a tendency to pronounce about problems such as marriage and divorce in generalized 'Christian' terms, and then, when accused of departing from our tradition, to reply loftily that we must never suppose that we have the Lord's *actual words*. So, insensibly, the Church's teaching seems to be edging further and further away from the spirit, not only the letter, of the New Testament. No wonder then if there is a rigorist backlash, returning to a literal interpretation of particular texts.

What is a moral theologian to do, who cannot take the necessary time to become a biblical theologian without giving up being a moral theologian? How, as a non-expert, can one actually use the Bible for moral guidance, general or detailed? This needs to be put even more urgently: What does the authority of Christ mean now in practice? The question I am trying to ask is quite a naïve one. It amounts to this: How can we, as twentieth-century Christians, use these sources to help us to find out what the Lord actually wants us to do? I am making the assumptions that we have a living Lord, that he has preferences now which claim our loyalty and that the Bible has some role for us in finding out what these are.

BIBLE AND CHURCH

Professor James Barr has said, 'the Bible furnishes the classic primitive model for the understanding of God'.[1] He has noted the paradox of the paramount importance of the Bible but the difficulty today about using it, and stated firmly that his 'own position is in every respect in favour of a greater and freer use of the Bible by the church'. He believes that 'many of the troubles of modern

39

Christianity are self-inflicted burdens which would be much lightened if the message of the Bible were more highly regarded'.[2]

Heartened by this scholarly optimism, we may hope to find that biblical criticism will prove a help rather than a threat. First, one does well as a non-expert to learn two precepts from the biblical scholars. The first of these is to extend the textual critics' rule, 'prefer the harder reading', and apply it to one's whole effort to understand biblical teaching. It just will not do, if one is trying to see how biblical data can help people to make moral decisions, to say at the first inconvenience 'That must be an interpolation'. There is no kind of integrity in taking only the bits one likes and building a moral system out of them.

So are we to have only the bits we do *not* like? There is no need to be depressed. We have lost the comfort of proof-texts that put our minds to sleep, but what we keep is the stimulus of an alarm bell to wake us up. The minimum honest interpretation of scripture includes the lesson that the Lord is apt to have surprises in store.

But still this approach, rigidly applied in its turn, could simply lead back into a literalism of the awkward bits. It needs to be controlled by the second precept, that Bible and Church are not to be taken apart. There needs to be a constant insistence that the Bible is the Church's book.[3] Whatever we believe about inspiration, the books of the New Testament were written by early Christians in particular situations. The Church was there first and the scriptures emerged from it under God's guidance, as Christians believe. To quote Professor Barr again: 'The Pauline letters are letters from the apostle to the churches, not letters from God to St Paul'.[4] What the New Testament does is take us back to the early days of the Church, near to its foundation: not bypass it and give us a clear window into the will of God.

'Scripture' is not something to be separated from the Communion of Saints. To read the Bible on one's own in small doses and try to apply it straight to twentieth-century life is asking for trouble. To read it in the company of the Church as the book of the Church, the Church of the first Christians, the Church through the centuries and the Church of today's scholars, is to give it the chance to supply the sustenance one needs. When one is struggling with an ethical problem, one can hope in all diffidence to find that the biblical writings can be a kind of means of grace. Besides hoping for God's grace, one is summoning up the grace of one's fellow Christians who have trodden this way before. The way they have found to express their beliefs is part of an available heritage. We need proof-texts less if we understand that what Jesus did and said is, as C. F. Evans put it in 1963, 'refracted through the experience of those who, by using what he did and said, had come to apprehend more of what he was to them'.[5]

To say that the Bible is a kind of means of grace is a way of saying that it can nourish people as the sacraments nourish them. It builds them up as members of the Body of Christ, not characteristically as lone individuals. To shift the metaphor to a different kind of upbuilding, the use of the Bible is supposed to be edifying. These metaphors of growth and construction are more useful for our present purpose than metaphors of enlightenment for people who seldom see a slow dawn and are used to electric switches. We ought not generally to expect instant illumination from reading the Bible but a gradual, sometimes imperceptible, shaping of a recognizable new creation.

It is common ground among Christians that the God in whom we believe gives us enough to go on. So there develops the temptation to look for a definitely grounded infallibility: an infallible Bible for Protestants, an infallible Church for Catholics. But after all there is no need to suppose that the Holy Spirit proceeds by dictation, whether to evangelist or Pope. In studying the New Testament we find ourselves among fallible and inspired Christians of the first century, while today we are among fallible and inspired Christians of the twentieth.

The question for everybody, Protestant or Catholic, sceptic or simple believer, is where to put one's trust. If as a Christian one is able to say 'Trust God', His will has to be ascertained. In practice, one has to trust people. We have Church and Bible because people have trusted other people to interpret the will of God to them. Some have trusted blindly, some with caution, trusting and doubting and trusting again, like trying the ice to see if it will bear.

THE AUTHORITY OF CHRIST

Where does all this come to rest? We cannot all trust other people, and the other people yet others, for ever. Again it is common ground among Christians that the person to be trusted is Christ. Does this mean that the special kind of inspiration that we cannot ascribe either to Pope or evangelist, we do ultimately ascribe to the Lord himself? To call him 'infallible in faith and morals' is dangerous when human beings are so ready to dogmatize on his behalf, and when all we know of him and his teachings comes from fallible human beings; but it does indicate something which I believe ultimately needs to be affirmed. Such affirmation of the authority of Christ is part of the problem, not part of the answer. It will certainly not make moral decision quite straightforward, only more urgent.

We still cannot read of God's will from the teaching in the Gospels, even when it seems as direct as 'What God has joined, let not man put asunder'.

There are three reasons for this. First, even when people believe that they know the very words of the Lord, there are still plenty of arguments about how his teaching was and is to be applied. Second, we cannot claim to have the whole truth and nothing but the truth about what he said; though on the principle of taking the hardest reading we cannot deny that he gave some stern teaching about marriage and divorce. Third, there is more to be said about his authority in the light of the realization that although he is our Lord he was none the less a man of the first century.

We may and should say that his own age, his own time and place, formed his mind, that he truly was 'conditioned' by his own circumstances: that is part of what incarnation means, not a contradiction of incarnation. Then we may add that to condition is not the same as to mislead; to shape need not be to distort. If there was indeed a perfect man, he was one who responded perfectly to the conditions of his age, not one who belonged to no age at all. At least there is a complex interplay between the divine and the human. We cannot assume that the Incarnate Lord could take a 'God's eye view' of the whole of human history and speak to us in the twentieth century as directly as he spoke to his own contemporaries. So we cannot base an argument upon infallibility. What we start with is a moral authoritativeness which convinced people then and still convinces today. 'Never man spake as this man.' One wants to be on his side, even when he utters hard sayings.

What he points to is a kingdom and a heavenly Father to whom he is totally obedient. So far, so human. But now the old argument 'Either God or not a good man' begins to bite. Its bite is twofold. On the one hand, there are hints already that the humanity of Christ, though real, is not the whole truth about him. His relationship with the Father, the effect he made upon his contemporaries, his controlled power, his preaching of repentance without himself showing any sense of sin yet without giving the impression of hypocrisy, all suggest something special and even uncanny about him. There are indications that something greater than Solomon is here. A claim is being made, not just for respect but for allegiance. We cannot just settle down to admire.

On the other hand, we cannot in any case settle down to admire, because everything went wrong. He required people to take sides and they took sides against him. His horrible death and the ruin of the hopes that had been placed in him are among the certainties of history.

The vindication which follows is on the other side of real failure. If we believe in the Resurrection, that is the basis for acknowledging the authority of Christ. He is vindicated as crucified and risen: the one does not confer authority without the other. His death shows that whatever he stands for, he stands for to the limit: nothing makes him draw back. His rising shows that whatever he stands for is not defeated: he has not avoided disaster but broken through it. The death and rising are parts of one story which stands or falls as a whole.

If this account is sound, our beliefs about how loyal Christians ought to behave must be based upon the whole story rather than on attempts to tease out the details of Christ's teaching. Both the fundamentalism that bandies proof-texts and the liberalism that slides cheerfully over the surface of New Testament teaching look like equally inadequate notions of Christian obedience. Our present Christian duty may or may not be straightforwardly linked with particular passages in Gospels or Epistles. If it is to be *Christian* duty, it must be linked somehow with the Cross and Resurrection of Christ. Its keyword is 'therefore': the characteristic 'therefore' of St Paul.

For God has not destined us for wrath, but to obtain salvation through our Lord Jesus Christ, who died for us. . . . *Therefore* encourage one another and build one another up.[6]

Welcome one another, *therefore*, as Christ has welcomed you, for the glory of God.[7]

And especially:

Therefore God has highly exalted him and bestowed on him the name which is above every name, that at the name of Jesus every knee should bow.[8]

This surely is the greatest 'ought' that ever came from an 'is'. It is the proper background to all Christian ethical thinking.

WHAT FOLLOWS?

So the most practical way to set about using the New Testament is to immerse oneself in the whole story, not separating out chosen details but letting them take their place in the total picture. I think this can mean something quite definite. It means that the question one will mainly be asking is 'How does what I propose to do look in the light of the Cross and Resurrection? Is following this policy or impulse the sort of thing I can do in the sight of the Lord who triumphed in that particular way?'

To ask this question is not to lose touch with the Lord's teaching, because the Lord who died and rose is also the Lord who lived and taught; and surely we know a good deal about what he taught. To take seriously what we are told he said, in its context, can be a promising way of trying to find out what he now asks of us, provided that we are wary of proof-texts and try to eschew debating points; and provided that we remember all along that what we actually have before us is what our fellow-Christians have said. The words of Christ are handed on and interpreted by the Christian community; and they have to be applied by the Christian community today, in the wider community of all our contemporaries.

Thirty years ago it seemed straightforward to take one's stand on the conviction that in the matter of divorce we truly 'have the mind of Christ', and a rigorist mind at that. According to Christ's teaching, it appeared, there could simply be no such thing as divorce for Christians: 'Whoever divorces his wife and marries another, commits adultery against her, and if she divorces her husband and marries another, she commits adultery'. On this simple understanding of the data, attempted remarriage is really living in sin: excommunication is more to the point than Church blessings. To avoid this harsh conclusion, much play was made with the possibility that some marriages had not been joined together by God and might be put asunder. Legal loopholes were welcome, especially biblical ones. Did St Paul allow divorce for desertion when he laid down that an unbelieving partner might be allowed to depart?[9] Did the Lord himself in St Matthew's Gospel allow divorce for adultery: 'saving for the cause of fornication'?[10] The trouble was that *porneia* did not mean 'adultery'; and that in any case responsible Christian thought was coming, not by picking and choosing but by scholarship and common sense, to give more weight to the account in St Mark's Gospel. Here is a place where biblical criticism has tightened, not loosened, the strictness of the teaching. The plain prohibition of divorce in Mark is surely more basic than the 'Matthaean exception', whatever exactly the exception originally meant. It looks as if even in the early Church the search for loopholes in the 'hard sayings' had begun; or, to put it more gently, the search for ways of understanding and applying the tradition of the words of the Lord had started even before the New Testament was completed.

If the loopholes fail us, is rigorism the right answer? It is needful to take it seriously, not from a fundamentalist belief in the verbal inerrancy of scripture, but because it is clear that Christ challenged and even upset his immediate followers by the uncompromising character of his teaching about divorce. A liberalism that does not challenge or upset anybody is not a Christian liberalism.

But rigorism is not the answer. In its determination to be safe rather than sorry it ignores the whole for the sake of a part. Rigorism as a version of Christian ethics is so one-sided as to be almost self-contradictory, when the whole thrust of the Gospel teaching is so markedly towards mercy and the availability of forgiveness, and the Lord himself came into conflict with the religious leaders of his day precisely for sitting so lightly to their kinds of rigorism. If we know anything about Jesus, we know that he refused to be tied up in legalistic bonds. If a serious attempt to apply his teaching leads straight into an unmerciful severity or a legalistic casuistry, we cannot have got it right. It is simple enough to quote 'Whoever divorces his wife and marries another, commits adultery against her' as a proof that there is really no such thing as divorce, that marriage is indissoluble. But when this wife has run away with another man and is longing to be divorced, is her forsaken husband to be debarred for ever in the name of the Gospel from comfort and company? When two immature young people thought their attraction would last for ever and find, once they have had their white wedding, that they have nothing in common, must we say that God has joined them, or make them prove to a church court that He has not, and all this for the sake of Christ? But if we cannot believe that marriages are 'indissoluble' in a metaphysical or a legal sense, what are we to do with the hard sayings?

As rigorism was the obvious answer to begin with, so next the obvious answer looks like a special demand laid upon the followers of Christ, who know what they are taking on. When it turns out that unyielding rigorism can hardly be applied to everyone, it seems natural to apply it to church members only, creating a double standard no more merciful and potentially more priggish than universal severity: 'Let the rest of the world do what it will, we loyal ones have our holy law which we will not abandon!' But that is just what the Pharisees said, to their credit and ruin. It is defeatist to acquiesce in such a limitation of the scope of God's will. Nor does rigorism always work even where we think it should. When it turns out that Christians are not immune to matrimonial disaster, there burgeons after all a legalistic casuistry which studies the possibilities of nullity or distinguishes, somewhat irrelevantly, 'innocent' and 'guilty' parties. It is no wonder that these hard or narrow views have been opposed by a soft liberalism which urges the kind of compassion that lives 'in the spirit' of Christ's teaching without ever doing anything differently on account of it.

It is worth not merely admitting but emphasizing the unattractiveness of all the alternatives by which we have seemed to be confronted. However messy our present situation, it is surely a matter of solid gain that all these approaches, rigorism, the double standard, and plain liberalism, now seem discredited, or at least much weakened. It would be over-optimistic to assert that the Christian Church now has a clearly articulated view to put in their place; but if one believes that a better understanding is available, is biblical, is increasingly carrying conviction, and is in fact the rationale behind what the Church is trying to do in this difficult matter, it is worth trying to make this better view explicit.

To deny that there is such a thing as divorce at all defines away the real sin of putting asunder what God has joined.[11] A broken marriage is not a contradiction but a disaster, an unnatural smashing of what was built to last, an amputation inflicted upon a living body. The bond of marriage cannot be neatly untied, only harshly severed. When this injury has already happened the question is how the wound can best be healed, and the temptations are either to cover it up soothingly at risk of its festering, or to set about keeping it open for ever as a proof of one's own integrity.

Divorce may happen, but it is a desperate necessity rather than an ordinary contingency. When the question is put in terms of indissolubility, we can say that marriage is characteristically indissoluble. The intention of permanence is built into its meaning. We have to admit that its indissolubility is what the lawyers call 'defeasible'.[12] The question 'Is marriage indissoluble or is it not?' is like 'Can you manage without your right hand?'[13] To reply 'Yes' or 'No' will mislead. 'Of course not' is the proper, instant answer. My right hand is as much needed, and as much my own, as anything I have; but it remains true that people have had, and survived, amputations. It would be foolish to live in a state of readiness for such a wretched contingency, imagining every cut finger turning to blood poisoning, finding out about artificial limbs, adjusting myself to the idea. But if it did come to that, I should have to do the best I could, and other people would have to do what they could to help, even if the loss had been my own fault. The comparison emphasizes the emergency character of divorce, its hurt and distress; and more positively it gives a clue to the ordinariness and proper reliability of the 'one-flesh union'.

When we look again at the teaching we find in the New Testament, the double-standard theory of strict rules for church members and tolerance for everyone else seems to be the least promising way of interpreting it. It is hard to believe that in this one instance Jesus fell in with the human longing to tidy everything up with laws. The way the story is told in St Mark's Gospel rings true. It is easy to believe that when he was questioned about divorce Jesus talked positively about marriage and took the whole question back behind the law of Moses to the Creation. The centre of the whole matter is that husband and wife shall become one. From this, much follows: but what follows is not after all either rigorism or a new and special law for Christians, but the basic *unnaturalness* of divorce.

Into this positive understanding of a human tendency, blessed by God, to form 'pairbonds', to vow faithfulness to each other for life and be each other's chosen and fit companions, the hard sayings fit as vivid, characteristic, maybe hyperbolic utterances of the Lord. If on the contrary we take the hard sayings as primary and try to make them the foundation for a new Christian law of marriage, they neither fit with the rest of the Gospel nor yield a credible practical policy. It is significant that one of the contexts in which Christ's teaching on marriage and divorce is presented is the Sermon on the Mount. Surely 'Everyone who divorces his wife . . . makes her an adulteress' does indeed belong alongside 'Everyone who looks at a woman lustfully has already committed adultery with her in his heart' and 'If anyone strikes you on the right cheek, turn to him the other also'. These are neither vague ideals to be ignored nor legislation to be enforced, though Christians have taken them in the one way or the other. They are crisp characterizations of a way of living. We still have the problem the early Church already had, of translating these insights into policy, to help one another put them into practice and rescue one another when things go incurably wrong.

– 6 –

Beyond fairness

But the fruit of the Spirit is love, joy, peace, patience, kindness, goodness, faithfulness, gentleness, self-control.

St Paul, Galatians 5.22–23

NATURAL LAW

We have been collecting some pieces of a jigsaw. The question is to put them together into a recognizable Christian picture. What we have spread out in front of us are, first, the conviction that God's will is fundamentally good for us; second, the notion of the 'pair-bond' as in some way a human 'norm' and fidelity as a deep human need; third, the understanding that Christian ethics cannot be trivial or easy if the Cross is basic to the Christian faith; fourth, the belief that the Lord gave some definite teaching about marriage which was felt to be hard to keep; and fifth, the certainty that when this teaching is interpreted legalistically something has gone wrong.

The simplest way to put these pieces, or most of them, together is by way of the time-honoured, and at present unfashionable, idea of natural law. Talk about norms suggests just that. What else is a norm but a law of human nature? When people call marriage a 'gift of God' they mean that it belongs to our creation, according to God's good purpose. So we can retain the urgency of the 'law of Christ' without ascribing to his teaching an uncharacteristic legal rigidity. The Lord was not promulgating a new edict against divorce, but recalling people to what marriage is meant to be. The law of faithful monogamous marriage matters because it is designed for human happiness. This is not legalism but realism. God's grace is there to help us; and if we fail His mercy will enable us to go on again.

This cannot be the whole story, but it is an essential part of the whole story. At its best, the idea of natural law bases morality on what is good for us. It would be a pity to refuse to give it a hearing because it has been misused. Natural law has had some harsh and rigid interpretations, especially in sexual ethics, but the core of it is the notion that there is reason behind the universe and that human fulfilment has to do with the way we are made. Of course it is controversial, some people would say naïve, to think in such a definite way about human nature: but such belief is really just a summary of the doctrine of creation without being fundamentalist about Adam and Eve.

What has put a good many liberal-minded people off the whole idea of natural law has been the way in which moralists have taken it upon themselves to use it to read off a biased 'ought' from a selected 'is'. For instance, they have deduced the wickedness of contraception from the ordinary fertility of sexual union. That is not what the idea of natural law ought to be doing for us. It is properly a kind of constant reminder that morality has a point.

The strength of this way of assembling our data around the notion of what is good for us is that the teaching in the Gospels is not made to look like arbitrary commandments laid upon believers. At least we can get rid of the persistent notion that there are two standards: a sort of honours degree and pass degree in goodness. God's will is for the whole of humanity, not only for religious people. The teaching of Christ is not an extra demand, whether optional or compulsory, upon his own followers but a return to fundamentals. So Christians may well diagnose the moral troubles of today as caused by departure from the law of God, but this need not make them anti-humanist. They share with their contemporaries the goal of making people happy by finding out what truly is good for them.

So the concept of 'natural law' as the law of our creation starts well by making positive sense of the lifelong union of a man and a woman. But when union fails, the 'hard sayings' about marriage and divorce still stand out. Are we to force them into place, or try to complete the puzzle without them? If all putting asunder is contrary to God's loving purpose for us, can a Christian ever have anything to do with divorce at all? Should Christians try to have the law tightened up, or at least assume that disciples of Christ will never need it? If on the other hand there is nothing in our teaching to make anyone ever want to say 'If such is the case of a man with his wife, it is not expedient to marry',[1] is our interpretation just a dilution and ought we to go back to rigorism?

It is all very well to affirm that the problem ought never to arise because God's grace is always available. Some people find this well-meaning insistence positively unhelpful. It sounds odd to say that grace can be over-emphasized, but the point is that it can easily be presumed upon. Christians cannot turn on a tap for help to gush out. The way of the Cross may include the experience of God's absence. The dogged affirmation of the availability of grace makes

49

keeping the natural law sound unnaturally easy. There are large numbers of people, including Christian believers, whose real miseries cannot be fitted into such a clear picture. It is just complacent to assert that if they tried harder or prayed harder they would surely find the help they need to avoid matrimonial shipwreck. The real world is not like that. The followers of Christ still have to make bleak practical choices between prohibitions and permissions. To make sense of his hard sayings we must take the puzzle partly to pieces and put it together again.

LONGEST WAY ROUND

The Christian starting-point is still the presupposition that the puzzle will fit together, that the teaching of the Lord will make sense and that the accounts we have of it are not distorted beyond all recognition. On this standing-ground we can afford to confront head on the alarming idea that sometimes the teaching just is too hard to be kept, and worse, that it is *not fair* to expect people to keep it. Everyone but the most austere rigorist, surely everyone who has seen beloved relatives or friends go through marital breakdown, can produce convincing evidence for allowing divorce and even remarriage: in other words, for not taking the hard sayings at their face value. We simply cannot believe that all remarried people are 'living in sin'. Sometimes we feel sure that they have found the positively best answer in the circumstances.

So is the teaching of Christ unfair or unrealistic? Unpalatable ideas are better faced than avoided. Let us roundly affirm that the teaching of Christ is not what we call fair. The whole point of it is that it transcends fairness and takes us into a world where we stop being obsessed by our rights. 'If anyone would sue you and take your coat, let him have your cloak as well.' No system of justice could possibly be founded on precepts like this; and 'Whoever marries a divorced woman commits adultery' is on the same footing.

Neither liberal nor rigorist can cope with these demands. The liberal is apt to resort to talk about ideals. It would be nice if people lived up to the standards Christ put before us, but we cannot really expect it when circumstances are adverse. Rigorism is tougher. The rigorist takes the divorce sayings, and often, be it noted, only the divorce sayings, and rather than let them go by default makes the misconceived attempt to enforce them. Second marriages, even after many years, are supposed to be treated as literally adulterous. Rigorism, in fact, is a short cut. It sees the right destination, faithful monogamy, and wants everyone to head straight for it, ignoring the difficulties of the terrain, with very little help to offer to people who come to grief.

The true answer, which will never be reached if the difficulty of the question is denied, must be that the kind of faithfulness through thick and thin which is expected of people who follow Christ is a *harvest* of a whole way of life.[2] Christian perfection is a 'fruit of the Spirit', not something attainable piecemeal by law-keeping. We could have learnt from St Paul, what experience is always teaching us, that beyond certain limits law-keeping and law-enforcement work havoc with the demand for love. Yet the demand for love is there all the time and the Gospels press it upon us. The only way is to grow the harvest first and then reap it. So any particular problem such as marriage and divorce is not on its own but opens up the whole question of God's kingdom and the possibility of human beings entering into it. We are still not talking about two standards, one for Christians and one for others, but of a way of living which in the last resort is our only hope. Love is compulsory in the same sense as food is compulsory: we shall starve without it.[3]

We can begin to see a kind of paradox about natural law: that the law of our being, which is what we were made for, is to become capable of going beyond law. So both letting us off and refusing to let us off are unsatisfactory ways of helping us to our destination. 'Christian standards' as often recommended look like legalism superimposed upon a lack of inspiration. It is time for the Church to stop nagging about morality, not in the name of permissiveness but in order to get a firmer grasp of the point of it all. There is a great deal of sowing and cultivating to be done before the harvest can be reaped. It is a besetting sin of moralists to pull up tender plants by the roots to see how they are getting on.

SHORTEST WAY HOME

It is no use expecting people to force themselves to be good. God does not seem to underwrite such attempts even when they are made in His name. More characteristically, He gives a glimpse of glory, at which people can be taken out of themselves and begin to respond. The Church is there to show people what there is to respond to, not to provide a substitute for response in the shape of rules and regulations, nor to excuse them from responding. As Austin Farrer excellently put it in a wedding sermon: 'The new miracle of Christ's religion is the union of duty and delight'.[4] To presume on this union is to nip the harvest in the bud. To say 'you ought to be grateful', whether for divine or human love, may be true but is nearly always

51

inept. It is a sure way to make people feel thoroughly ungrateful. Thankfulness has to be spontaneous or it fails or is false.

It would be defeatist to suppose that Christians have nothing distinctive to say about marriage; but there is no Gospel in depriving people of their just rights in the name of a kind of happiness which to them has proved a mirage. When people have not noticed any glory it is not reasonable to expect them to behave in heroic ways: when they have, what looks from outside like heroism can become natural.

Can a practical answer be found among all this 'on the one hand . . . on the other hand' of theory? It must be threefold. First, we need to take notice of the glimpses we have had so far and be ready to let them make a difference. Even a wobbly faith in a God who was killed and rose again begins to make both ordinary complacency and ordinary despondency look different. It is this difference which Christians need to communicate to their contemporaries, not alarmingly austere 'standards' that have to be kept up.

Second, we need to be less possessive about what there is to call out our response. Especially where we are concerned with marriage, there are plenty of glimpses of glory to be had which are not in any obvious way 'religious'. What people need is to be seized by a spirit which takes them out of themselves, whether they give 'spirit' a large or a small 's'. Romantic love can be as inspiring as piety and surely no less a gift of God. It can truly be something for human beings to build upon, not belittle.

Third, when the skies seem to have closed in and there are no glimpses of glory to be had, we must go for fairness, but not deceive ourselves that fairness can be more than an 'interim ethic'. It may be the best we can do, and is assuredly better than unfairness. So we have 'grounds of divorce', 'second chances', and all the legal and moral apparatus of trying to make the best of a bad job. If we have still, in many hundreds of years, not advanced beyond 'hardness of heart' we must be honest, like the law of Moses, and allow people their 'bills of divorcement'. When marriages have broken it is too late to preach indissolubility. Where divorce is unthinkable it is not because there is a law against it, but because people have positively found something better.[5] It is a cliché that still needs to be taken to heart that people must start where they are, not from somewhere before things went wrong. The Church has some responsibility for where people are, and therefore ought to do what it can, even belatedly, to give them the backing they need to build something solid among the ruins.

But then are we not to preach repentance, turning again? If we are to preach it in the name of the Lord we need to take care that we are not simply addressing victims rather than sinners, while the hardness of heart is our own. Above all, we can preach repentance only when we have some idea of what we think we mean by saying that 'the kingdom of heaven is at hand'. Turning again needs a new direction for turning to. It cannot be a condition of repentance that people should remain permanently stranded in their irrevocable history. What we have to do is pick up the pieces as best we may.

Christians as individuals and the churches to which they belong cannot opt out of deciding what 'picking up the pieces' may mean. The moral and legal arguments about divorce go on and on and still cannot be abandoned. We owe it to the people who have suffered the breakdown of their marriages to find out what we can do for them and their children. There is a lot of listening to be done before the Christian churches can hope to offer much convincing succour to the casualities of matrimonial shipwreck. Rigorism has given people the idea that Christians cannot be expected to understand their miseries. Meantime liberalism has concentrated on the woes of unfortunate lovers and has often forgotten the most innocent victims of unhappy marriages, the children who have to accept the upheaval of their lives and the loss of beloved parents in the name of a scarcely-understood grown-up fulfilment. There is a new feeling about, a willingness to try to find out where the shoe pinches and why after all Christians believe that divorce matters.[6] It is not good enough just to be against it, like the famous preacher about sin. Faith in Christ ought to suggest that he was truly on the side of muddled humanity and showing us what belongs and what does not belong to our well-being.

HARVEST OF THE SPIRIT

Even while we go on with the argument it is not too late to put it in proportion. There is more to Christian morality, and more to the Christian understanding of marriage, than unhappiness, sin and sorrow. It is not at all too late to talk about the meaning of marriage positively, and even to use it as an example, on a human scale, of what is the meaning of 'response'. A good marriage is something of which we do have an idea; and it can truly give a glimpse of what it is like to get beyond the claiming and conceding of rights, and at the same time beyond the dogged performance of duties, into a world where people enter wholeheartedly into each other's joys and troubles.

Human life is full of good examples of the morality of response, but usually this kind of 'transcendence' is an optional extra. Our hearts go out to another human being and we do something kind which could never reasonably be expected of us. The reason why marriage is a special case, and indeed a pattern case, is that the kindness and goodness can be expected. There is no room for neutrality in marriage: one can hardly be a fairly good wife. It is a duty to go beyond duty. So the paradox of what is required of husbands and wives matches, and illuminates, the paradox of what is required of Christians. Loving somebody else 'as oneself' is not heroism or even virtue but something that begins to happen of its own accord or not at all.

Part of what the unity of marriage means is that we can understand how the boundaries of self-interest can be redrawn.[7] I really cannot distinguish my happiness from yours. Husbands and wives are not immune from being inconsiderate to one another, impatient with one another, furious with one another. They may misunderstand what the other is trying to explain. But the context within which they are operating is that they belong to each other so that 'we' is at least as real as 'I' and 'I'. To fall in love, and better still to live together through a whole life, is to have a much less overpowering notion of what is good for me as opposed to what is good for you. Because we can see for ourselves that this is the way that many married people unselfconsciously live their lives, we can take heart that the hard sayings of the Lord are not impossible either, if only there is something to take us out of ourselves. Doggedly to set oneself to live up to one's highest ideals is asking for trouble; but one can find oneself in a position where one has forgotten to be selfish.

What we need is not 'situation ethics' of the shallow kind, which seems to deny that there are any laws at all. We are not looking for what used to be called in the 1960s a 'new morality'. It is an old morality, which human beings including Christians constantly seek and fall short of: a morality of loving others as oneself. To have any hope of achieving this we need grace, heavenly and earthly. We build each other up in our human relationships and find ourselves able to achieve by response what we could never manage by duty. So at least we have made a start. It is not a pointless paradox to say that the real law of our nature is to go beyond law.

But is there any merit in doing what we ought when it comes naturally to us? That is exactly the point. There are human situations, of which marriage and parenthood are the clearest examples, in which merit becomes irrelevant because what we want to do and what we ought to do begin to coincide. We can pick up the ordinary commonplace notion of doing something 'with a good grace' and revive its faded meaning. Being able to do something for someone else with a good grace is, precisely, to bring forth the fruit of the spirit:[8] quite contrary to the grimly dutiful striving of 'justification by works'. To live according to the teaching of Christ is not difficult: it is either impossible or easy. To see in everyday life that human beings both need, and can be capable of, this kind of 'transcendence' is to begin to discover the possibility of a way of living which might be dignified by the name of a morality of generosity.

A morality of generosity is not really as far as one might suppose from utilitarianism, the belief in the 'greatest happiness of the greatest number'. Christians on the whole are afraid of utilitarianism for the wrong reasons. They look on it as unprincipled and irreligious and do little justice to the ethical fervour of thoroughgoing utilitarians for the best outcome. A morality of generosity, learnt unselfconsciously by response not by precept, could pick up this sense of the importance of happiness, with a more exuberant, less calculating emphasis. Generosity has no need to think of people as units and do sums with them. It can value happiness without constantly asking 'what's the harm?'

Meanwhile rights and duties are as valid as ever and when they are denied they may become desperately important. Any notion that generosity either promises or threatens to abolish rights and duties is cruelly unrealistic. To learn to transcend rights is not the same thing as to ride roughshod over them. If the deserted wife is unscrupulously abandoned without even getting her 'bill of divorcement' it is too soon to preach that marriage is a mystical union. Indeed, one way of understanding the Gospel teachings on divorce is to realize that the Lord takes the side of vulnerable people whose rights are not being acknowledged. Maybe 'putting asunder' is forbidden more because an easy divorce law is apt to inflict miserable wrong upon women, than because marriage is some kind of metaphysical bond.

A generous attempt to understand what is really good for people will avoid the notorious kind of double standard which lets the strong always win and the weak always lose. But conversely, generosity will also be wary of that plausible moralism which stands the double standard on its head and presents all duties as mine and all rights as yours. To be inexorably strict with myself and give you everything you want is not much better than the reverse. To take other people's good to heart is to give imaginative respect to their duties as well as to their rights. It is ungenerous and thoughtless to assume that it is quite all right for other people to give way to immediate impulses in the name of sexual fulfilment while we few, in our virtue, have to be chaste.

Generosity will not be quick to assume either that one is quite different from everyone else or that people are all alike. Of course it is tempting, especially in sexual ethics where feelings are so strong, to treat oneself as a special case: what I want must be God's will because I want it so much. But it is even more tempting, especially in sexual ethics where other people's feelings are often so incomprehensible, to generalize dogmatically from one's own experience: to blame other people for claiming rights which matter to them but do not interest me, or for succumbing to temptations which I happen not to have felt.

To find our way through these thickets the best clue is still to ask what can be done now to fulfil rather than distort people's variegated humanity: in other words, what harvest, human and divine, can they hope to reap. All this is easier to assert than to establish, especially when all kinds of damaging things have already happened. What this way of thinking has to offer is not recipes for success but glimpses of what success is like, for us to keep in view and steer by.

– 7 –

Sacrament

My marriage was the most fortunate event of my life.

Edwin Muir, *An Autobiography*

CHRISTIAN DISTINCTIVENESS?

The conviction that Christ was not legislating about something called 'Christian marriage', but recalling his disciples to the meaning of marriage for human beings 'from the beginning of creation', is not soft or permissive; but softness and permissiveness can be a way that this emphasis risks taking. The danger is a gradual slipping away from anything the early Christians could have recognized as the Gospel which so enthralled them. The early Church did have new standards and a way of living which distinguished it from the world around. It must have looked quite rigorist. How dare we be so 'liberal' as to suggest that after all there is not much difference between Christians and others and that really we are all feeling our way together? What has happened to the consciousness of being 'in Christ' which is supposed to make the whole difference to all our natural relationships?

One answer is to say 'What indeed?' and make that the point. Until we really are reaping the harvest we cannot expect to have the fruit to eat. Without some understanding of the health of the whole body there is not much we can do by tinkering about with the symptoms. But if that were all we could say about how Christianity stands today, we should be needlessly defeatist. Nearly two thousand years of preaching the Gospel has made a difference. We are not a tiny group of new converts living in a self-sufficient pagan world.

Contemporary attitudes to many questions, including marriage, have been shaped by Christian teaching. Our distinctiveness has been blurred, not entirely by being lost but to a great extent by being shared. It is generally more accurate to regard ourselves as Pharisees, upholders of a great tradition and tempted to possessiveness, than as early Christians with a brand new message to deliver.

57

The Christian Gospel is nearly two thousand years old. It has been both cherished and betrayed in every generation. It may be difficult to be sure which of these is which, but we have to try. In a time like the present, when we have the feeling that we are accelerating through history, it is a major task to come to terms loyally with traditional certainties and their traditional formulations. Can we say the same things as earlier Christians did, and in what words?

Christians have often expressed their distinctive conviction that marriage is in some way holy by calling it a sacrament. Catholics made it one of the seven sacraments. The Reformers expressly denied that matrimony is a 'sacrament of the Gospel' in the sense in which Baptism and the Eucharist are.[1] It is neither 'ordained by Christ himself' nor 'generally necessary to salvation'.[2]

Yet the sacramental character of marriage is a tenacious notion. The solemnity of the marriage service invites the notion that a Christian wedding is a sacrament, even if it is not on a level with a christening or a service of Holy Communion. Even Protestant Christians, when they want a clinching argument against the possibility of divorce, will say as if it were something we all knew, 'But marriage is a sacrament'. What they are apt to mean is 'How can we ever break these vows and undo this joining of hands?' But the theory that marriage is a sacrament is not particularly about weddings at all.

The idea has a complicated history, going back to St Paul. In the Epistle to the Ephesians[3] the 'one flesh' union between a man and a woman is described as 'a great mystery' (*sacramentum*) and a sign of Christ's love for the Church. Much has been built on this: sometimes inspiringly, and sometimes so legalistically as to bring the whole idea of marriage as sacramental into disrepute. Yet this way of thinking theologically about marriage has plenty of life in it yet and needs sorting out rather than explaining away.

There are two confusions about the holiness of marriage to be rejected here. One of them ought to be obvious. It is a fallacy to argue that because marriage signifies 'the mystical union that is betwixt Christ and his Church' divorce must be simply impossible, not just wrong. One might as well argue that because a wedding ring given and received is a symbol of the union between husband and wife, to lose one's wedding ring must be impossible, not just careless. A symbol can be more fragile than the reality it signifies without being meaningless. What the argument should say is: This symbol has a real and deep significance. It is irreverent to treat it casually. It ought to be treasured; but treasuring the sign should not mean idolizing it. If two people are miserable, it is pointless to make them stay together as if they were somehow threatening the union of

Christ with his Church. There are plenty of better arguments against divorce than this.[4]

Second, the holiness of marriage for Christians is not explained but confused when people try to make marriage fit into a definition of a sacrament as a sign instituted by Christ. They formalize the conviction that what Christ said and did surely makes all the difference into an assertion that Christ altered the meaning of marriage: he raised it to the status of a sacrament by teaching its indissolubility.[5] So 'Christian marriage' becomes something different in kind from the marriage of unbelievers. This way of thinking begins in enthusiasm and reverence and is too apt to end in tyranny and self-righteousness.

The Church of England's teaching has been both more realistic and, surely, more accurate. Marriage is indeed 'holy matrimony', not because Christ made it so but because it is what the Alternative Service Book calls 'a gift of God in creation'.[6] The true character of marriage goes back to 'the beginning'[7] and did not have to be added in later. What the teaching of Christ does is restore and illuminate it.

It is in line with this understanding that Article XXV of the Thirty-Nine Articles points out, polemically no doubt, that matrimony is not on the same footing as the 'two sacraments ordained of Christ our Lord in the Gospel, that is to say, Baptism, and the Supper of the Lord'. We can see that Baptism is a special sort of washing given to the Church and that the Eucharist is a special sort of eating and drinking. There is not in the same sense something called 'Christian marriage' which is a special sort of pairing. Christians have no right to colonize the marriage at Cana of Galilee as a Christian sacrament. It is worth reiterating that what 'Christ adorned and beautified with his presence' was a village wedding, celebrated with folk rites. The bride and bridegroom were presumably unbaptized and uninstructed in Christian theology, and were subject to a law which allowed the bridegroom to divorce his wife if he found 'some unseemly thing in her'. As Austin Farrer pointed out,[8] we are not told that the Lord preached to them their Christian duty: 'he saw to the supply of the wine'.

Whatever affirmations are to be made about miracles and about what kind of truth the author of St John's Gospel is trying to impart here, this story was recounted and believed of the Lord and must stay in the middle of what Christians understand about marriage: all the more so if its first hearers took its literal meaning for granted in order to explore other deep symbolic truths. Whatever we are supposed to learn from the story of the wedding at Cana about the wine of the Eucharist or the new wine of the Kingdom, the terms of reference and starting-point for all this exploration must be an ordinary human marriage.

HUMAN SIGN

What is left of the idea of the sacramental character of marriage when confusions adhering to it have been removed? Church of England children used to be taught in the catechism that a sacrament is 'an outward and visible sign of an inward and spiritual grace'. Without affirming that marriage is a sacrament, the Book of Common Prayer has given prominence at the beginning of the wedding service to the teaching in Ephesians about marriage being a sign. The human institution of marriage is able to show us something about 'the mystical union that is betwixt Christ and his Church'.

This is a sacramental way of thinking which presents marriage, not the rite but the way of life, as a natural symbol of divine reality. The union of a man and a woman is capable of bearing supernatural meaning: it is able to be a kind of parable of what Christians mean by the love of God. Karl Barth said that 'marriage is a sign and symbol representing fellowship between God and man'.[9]

The most straightforward significance, of course, is faithfulness, the faithfulness of Christ to his Church. This lesson seems plain enough to understand though it may not be so easy to put it into practice. It is no wonder, though it is a great waste, that in the attempt to prevail upon people to put it into practice its more negative moral implications have loomed large. But there is surely more to the mystery of the marriage bond than a new commandment, thou shalt not divorce; or even, be faithful as the Lord is faithful. This is the point at which to pick up again the idea that marriage, the human institution, gives positive glimpses beyond itself of some basic concepts of the Christian faith.[10] Especially the human pairbond can help to show the meaning of grace which need not dominate and unity which does not obliterate.

Some of the things Christians have always said about being made one with Christ and with each other are mysterious in the modern sense of puzzling as well as in the religious sense of transcendent. The fascinating but difficult theme of unity-in-plurality haunts Christian theology. Christians have been taught to make affirmations about the possibility of a kind of union which is not a confusion nor a blending, which is more than co-operation but more complex than mathematical oneness.[11] The doctrine of the Trinity sets forth three persons in one God; God is supposed to be in us and we in Him; the doctrine of Christ requires that Jesus should be one with God and yet a man, and that his death and resurrection somehow encompass us all; the doctrine of grace has encouraged us to believe that when God acts in us we are most truly ourselves. All these doctrines sound inspiring, but their meaning is not entirely obvious.

Christians say after St Paul 'not I, but Christ'; but they often say this dutifully and as it were politely. It may sound as if our own wills must simply be overcome if we are to come to any good; and then if we jib at being placed in this situation we are just rebellious. We know that for our wills to be made one with God's will we need grace; but the idea of grace can too easily be reduced to a kind of magic: we cannot do what we ought unless some power outside ourselves will steer us in a seemingly unnatural way.

What we need is not exhortation but explanation, and best of all practical illustration, of what can be meant by unity of will and especially of how it is thoroughly compatible with individual distinctness. In some human relationships, of which marriage is an especially clear example, these difficult sums are worked out for us. It is a fact that one can do more in someone else's power than one can in one's own and be more of a person, not less, as a result.

What happens quite ordinarily in marriage is that a common mind is formed over the years and strengthened by joint experience, so that a husband and wife can no longer identify their separate contributions. This is evidently so in the case of their material possessions; but it is just as true that their opinions and their whole style and approach to life are not able to be disentangled as belonging to one or the other. Sometimes one partner can be seen as dominating and the other as submitting.

> Belle my wife, she loves not strife,
> But she will lead me if she can;
> And to maintain an easy life
> I oft must yield, though I'm goodman.

More characteristically, and quite probably in the example quoted, the pattern is really much more complicated and it is true to say that husband and wife are forming each other. It soon ceases to make sense to ask, what would my life have been like if we had never met? One might as well ask, who would I be if I were someone else?

For many of us, the experience 'not I, but the grace of my husband or wife' is easier to identify than 'not I but Christ'. Marriage is a context in which grace can be rescued from being a rather claustrophobic technical term and take on a comprehensible human meaning. We do have some acquaintance with what it means for two wills to be united while still remaining two. To find one's will, not suppressed, but in harmony with the will of another, with love not merit, is something which millions of untheological husbands and wives have experienced at first hand.[12] Friendship can also illustrate the meaning of grace; but even close friends have their separate lives to lead, whereas married people may become one entity, even prosaically in the eyes of the law. The union of two lives in marriage might look like an impossibly demanding vocation, but it can be found to enable what it demands.

It should not be surprising that the sorts of things one is supposed to believe about God find echoes in the experience one already has of human life: that there are recurrent patterns in the way things are.[13] What we may hope for is a sort of double illumination,[14] by which ordinary marriage can be a ready-made analogy for divine grace, and conversely what we believe about God's grace lights up what marriage can be. Certainly in the passage in the Epistle to the Ephesians[15] about marriage and the unity of Christ with the Church it is not made entirely clear which way the argument is going. There is no reason why it should not go both ways, provided that what experience tells us about marriage is not simply confused with some people's experience of God.

We may start at the human end and use marriage as a parable, useful because it is something already familiar. Because as human beings we know what it is for two to be made one without losing their distinctness, we can begin to comprehend such ideas as 'not I but Christ'. Or we may begin at the religious end. Because some human beings have an awareness of being blessed by God they have an inner strength which we hope will show itself in their whole lives, including their marriages, so that their understanding of what is possible for human beings will be transformed. But if we try to put these two illuminations together and substitute for ordinary human marriage something called 'Christian marriage', exemplifying a special and religious kind of harmony already on the divine side of the comparison, we may be operating on a very high level, but our analogy between earthly and heavenly has disappeared.

MEANS OF GRACE

A sacrament is not only a kind of parable illuminating what we believe divine reality is like: it is also a *means* of grace. It is supposed actually to be a channel by which people are given the grace of God. Can marriage be a sacrament in this sense? The theory in the Church of Rome, somewhat obscured by the persistent emphasis on celibacy as a higher way, is that marriage, for Catholics, is just that: a means by which the couple impart God's grace to one another. Surely other

Christians can welcome this idea as true to the long-term experience of many Christian married people.[16] This is at least a far better way of maintaining that marriage is a sacrament than the defeatist assertion that marriage is so holy that people have got to put up with it however badly it turns out. If indeed it is possible for human beings to be ministers of grace mediating God's blessing to one another, surely husbands and wives may recognize each other as filling this priestly role, generally unconsciously and certainly unselfconsciously. When strength and encouragement come through marriage, a Christian will believe that this has something specific to do with the presence of God.

This sort of sacramentalism needs to be handled gently and tentatively for fear of brashness and presumption. There is no need to make loud announcements of the arrival of God's grace as if one were a back-slapping host at a party. Gratitude is more fittingly shown by recognizing and welcoming the human grace which is there in its own right as well as being the bearer of the divine blessing.

If we prefer to be reticent about God's grace and even put the notion aside for the present rather than seem to presume upon it, can sacramental ideas still illuminate the plain earthly reality of human marriage? 'Means of grace' is more than a dignified way of saying that we cheer each other up. To use this sacramental language about marriage is a way of putting a good emphasis upon our physical natures. The unity between husband and wife concerns 'one flesh', not only one spirit. Human beings 'make love' to one another. It is not a reluctant admission but a fundamental affirmation that what is physical is suitable to bear spiritual meaning.

The sacramental principle at its most basic is the idea that matter matters: that the physical is essentially the vehicle of the spiritual, not an irrelevant or unsatisfactory appendage to it.[17] That is why it is worth making the effort to go on talking this language and to clear away the misconceptions. The question is not whether there are two sacraments instituted by the Lord, or seven sacraments of which marriage is one, but whether the creation is all of a piece. Christians ought to find themselves at home in the recognition that the universe is sacramental through and through: 'God saw that it was good'; 'the Word was made flesh'; 'this is my body'. Everything human beings do, religious or secular, we do through our bodies. We express our variegated relationships with one another by bodily signs, by rising to our feet and shaking hands, by frowns and smiles, by respectful or affectionate kisses, and by the physical union which expresses the unity of a man and a woman. People kneel to pray, they join God's people by being washed and they are built up as members of His people by eating and drinking. So in keeping with all this, physical love-making can be comprehended as a human 'means of grace': not as an unworthy distraction nor as a be-all and end-all, but as the suitable expression of that complete commitment of a man and a woman to one another which is marriage.

This sacramental way of thinking is miles away from the notion of marriage as a churchly sacrament administered by a priest, a sort of licence for love, conferring respectability, under certain conditions, upon what would otherwise be illicit desires. The tenacity of that misconception has obscured the fact that it is the couple themselves who are the ministers of this sacrament. A marriage is made, humanly, legally, and theologically, by a man and a woman solemnly consenting to take each other for life. Witnesses are needed to establish the marriage as a public reality; but it has often been made clear that on a desert island without witnesses a man and a woman could truly marry one another. Whatever grace, human or divine, there is in marriage, that grace is conveyed by the spouses themselves, not by any other human being set up over them.[18]

– 8 –

Foundation fairness

In vain thy Reason finer webs shall draw
Entangle Justice in her net of Law
And right, too rigid, harden into wrong,
Still for the strong too weak, the weak too strong.

Alexander Pope, Essay on Man

THE PLACE OF LAW

Underlying the human and divine grace which we hope for and need, there is law which we take for granted. People who, with good reason, regard legalism as a great enemy may underestimate law. Flexibility is valuable by being incomplete. Freedom needs a framework. As Alice found in Wonderland, it is difficult to play croquet with flamingos for mallets. Even saints need laws in the shape of predictable and dependable regularities: rules of the road, procedures for making arrangements with one another and rites of passage for the milestones of life. Sinfulness makes it needful to add in all manner of limits and controls, civil courts to settle quarrels without resort to violence and all the apparatus of criminal justice to bring responsibility home to offenders.

The law of marriage and divorce is simply part of all this. From the ancient story of unfallen Adam saying to Eve 'This at last is bone of my bone and flesh of my flesh', to bridegrooms and brides today who say 'for better, for worse, for richer, for poorer, in sickness and in health', human beings have used words to inaugurate the union of husband and wife. Once society has become large and complex the words have to be laid down in advance so that it is plain when a marriage has really taken place. There has to be a body of law to define the meaning, the rights and the duties of 'marriage' in any particular community: to provide the structure within which individuals can hope to love and to cherish one another.

But also, much as we may deplore it, from ancient times[1] to the present there have been arrangements, more or less socially acceptable, by which people who found their marriages unbearable could legally extricate themselves. The most conspicuous difference today is not the availability of a law of divorce, but the fact that women have learnt to expect like consideration with men in the making, and the ending, of marriages.

Christians are naturally apt to look upon the divorce law as simply unsatisfactory and contrary to the will of God; though how they think that the law of Moses fits into the picture is not very clear. Ought Christians to feel guilty when as humane people they acquiesce in the legal ending of failed marriages, other people's or even their own? They are by no means the first of God's people so to acquiesce:[2] 'Moses because of the hardness of your hearts suffered you to put away your wives'.[3] The Mosaic law which made provision for divorces was surely not a strange piece of permissiveness cancelled at the first opportunity by the new law of Christ, but a safety-valve in case the worst should happen. Even a theocratic state needs arrangements for what is to be done when marriage bonds become intolerable. The formal 'bill of divorcement' is not a misunderstanding of God's will but a way of setting limits to unregulated human cruelty, just like the law of 'eye for eye, tooth for tooth'.

What a divorce judge is doing is pronouncing upon rights, and any society has to make up its mind what these rights shall be. More or less workable divorce laws can be based on many possible basic principles, unilateral repudiation, return of bride-price, matrimonial offence, irretrievable breakdown, mutual consent or, when the safety-valve is kept shut, wide-ranging nullity. It has not been found practicable by organized states either to forbid divorce entirely on the one hand, or on the other hand to leave matters of sex and the family entirely to people's private arrangements. The weak are likely to be better defended when some attempt is made to set limits to permissiveness and regulate people's expectations of one another. Yet the difficulty and paradox of trying to protect people against their natural protectors, their spouses or their parents, is such that a good family law is particularly hard to achieve.

It need not be Christian disloyalty to acknowledge these facts, to recognize the divorce law of one's own country as humanly valid, and maybe to work for a juster divorce law even at some risk of making divorce easier not harder. Christians have no more, and no less, right to say that the law of divorce is not their business than to say that the law of tort is not their business. They may well hope that going to law will never be part of their own lives; but some Christians, in an imperfect world, have characteristically concerned themselves with justice for other people.

THE LAW AND THE CHURCH

The history of Christian concern with the law of marriage and divorce is a sufficiently complex story that it lends itself to conflicting interpretations. To summarize it is to sketch out a case for a particular view by emphasizing one aspect or another.

If people believe that Christ was legislating, they may thoroughly approve of the control over marriage which the Christian Church has exercised for centuries in Christ's name. They will see traditional Christian rigorism as for everyone's good: a good which is now being lost as Christendom disappears and secularization takes over. So in God's name they oppose putting asunder. In some countries rigorists have had a good deal of success in keeping divorce impossible or difficult.

If it is claimed that Christ was indeed legislating, but only for disciples, it may on the contrary be seen as an advantage that the Church must now relinquish its hold upon people who accept no ecclesiastical authority, in order to speak all the more plainly to the faithful. Have Christians even done a wrong to their fellow human beings by interfering with their ordinary human rights?

For people who believe that the teaching of Christ was something quite different from legislation, the whole question of Christians and justice becomes more difficult. 'The Church deals in grace not law.' Was it simply a mistake for the Church to let itself become legalistically involved with matrimony? If Christians can sort out how to apply the teaching of Christ to believers, will they be in a position to take any particular line about whether the secular law of divorce ought to be strict or liberal? Should the Christian Church be counted as an 'interested party', with a right to lobby for its own particular point of view? What hope is there of Christians agreeing about what that point of view should be?

It is necessary to attempt a summary account of a suitable stance for Christians. It looks as if both taking over the legal system and opting completely out of it are mistakes. Human beings need laws, including laws about marriage, not as ends in themselves but as a foundation and framework for grace. When the Church takes over the law it seems to make it an end in itself to the detriment of grace. But to opt out may be to abandon responsibility and invite chaos. Because for many centuries the Church has taken part in people's marrying and giving in marriage, it has therefore taken on some responsibility for the way the law is. The interest the Christian Church has taken in the law of marriage and divorce has mostly been a duty, not a mistake. The work it still does in giving advice to the powers that be is a continuation of this duty rather than an interference. It can be part of 'dealing in grace' to make constructive suggestions about what legal framework would be the best basis for human happiness.

But this legal concern always carries with it the risk of misunderstanding. The greatest risk, which has unhappily not been avoided, is the risk of confusing law and grace, of wearing two hats as if they were one hat. So we have had a great deal of rigorism and then, in reaction, permissiveness. Either way, grace itself becomes legalized. If the Church's main business is seen as government, the mercy of Christ may go by default and the majesty of Christ may be shrunk to bureaucracy.

Christian advice is at its most valuable when church people are trying to make themselves useful, neither to dictate to secular society nor merely to accommodate to it. They believe that they have some insights about what is good for human beings: about faithfulness, stability and love. Christians have a proper concern, not a 'vested interest', in promoting the best conditions for human flourishing.

For a short while in this century there seemed to be a rare opportunity for churches to concentrate on their primary concerns because it seemed that legislatures were able and willing to do the lawmaking, while still taking heed of Christian opinion.[4] To say that the good opportunity has been squandered would be an exaggeration; but the state of affairs has deteriorated in various ways, some of them unnecessary. Liberal and rigorist opinion has become more polarized in ways which greater goodwill and clarity of mind could have prevented. Their differences ought to have been a matter of emphasis, allowing them still to speak with one voice to the outer world; instead of which Christian witness has become so confused and confusing that people with social and legal responsibility have not been given much help by the churches in comprehending the Christian point of view. It has to be said that the wrong criticisms have sometimes been made of recent developments.

WHERE NOW?

To criticize the law Christians need to understand the logic of the law. It is worrying that we now effectively have 'divorce by consent', but if we believe that marriages ought not to be kept in being if they can be shown to have broken down, what better evidence could there be for breakdown than the fact that both husband and wife want to part? It is shocking if legal aid is not made available for defending divorce cases, but again if the breakdown of the marriage is what counts, what kind of defence is envisaged once a suit has been filed? It is disturbing when people can obtain divorce by post, but once the upshot has become inevitable what is the use of prolonging their misery and requiring judges to sit in court to rubber-stamp their applications in the end?

Some of the checks and safeguards which critics of an easy divorce law would like to build into the law turn out in practice to increase bitterness, not to discourage divorce. Attempts to slow down divorces to make sure that breakdown has really occurred seem to be counter-productive. Instead of waiting calmly for statutory periods of separation to elapse and maybe discovering that the whole idea of divorce was a mistake, spouses merely choose the quicker and less pacific routes to their goal, intolerable behaviour or adultery, reliving in their petitions the worst moments of their marriages. How after all could a divorce law possibly aspire to 'buttress, rather than to undermine, the stability of marriage'?[5] The most that can reasonably be hoped is that it will not actually damage stability.

This is where criticism should rightly concentrate: upon the longer-term dangers of current policies. Hopes of saving faltering marriages may be unrealistic: but fears about future developments are only too realistic. If it is true, as we are continually told, that 'You can't put the clock back', the responsibility for the cumulative effect of changes is all the heavier. Even the removal of safeguards which have not proved their value has the positive effect of giving the green light to the behaviour the safeguards were intended to discourage.

Recent thinking on divorce law reform invites two complaints. First, reform seems to proceed piecemeal, with continual attempts to make things easier for individuals, without much thought of those other individuals who will suffer in the future from the assumptions now being allowed to take hold. Secondly, there is a short-term economy which refuses to consider arrangements which might be expensive, combined with a sort of bemused acceptance of the long-term costs, human and financial, of providing for the casualties of easy divorce. Is it after all so obvious that more judicial attention and even a larger element of 'inquest'[6] would be an unacceptable expense? The need for years of financial support for first wives and their children, when people act on the assumption that they have the right to a divorce, a new marriage and a second family, is at least an item to be weighed in the total account.

However strongly 'paternalism' is rejected, the law of marriage and divorce cannot help but have an educative role in forming the attitudes of people growing up and expecting to marry.[7] Many generations have looked on marriage as a more or less irrevocable step, not to be lightly taken in hand. It has not been quite true to say

'You can always get a divorce'. If that becomes evidently true, the consequences are not automatically predictable, but ought to be considered with as much seriousness as is rightly devoted to making divorce a less horrible experience for individuals.

Conservative criticism could be simplistic here in bandying about too easily the notion of 'divorce-mindedness'. Nobody thinks divorce is something desirable: until marriage has become miserable. Painless divorce does not make divorce attractive as such. What endangers the stability of marriage is not the availability of an escape-route but its predictable availability, as of right, at the sole behest of the spouses or even of just one spouse, so that marriage becomes a contract quite easy to terminate, and in course of time begins to be generally thought of in this way. The built-in expectation of stability around which married people can shape their lives may gradually become a dead letter. If their relationship founders, they are not answerable to anyone except their children. They need make out no case to anyone, not even to each other, for bringing their marriage to an end.

The logic of divorce law reform makes the legal definition of marriage as the voluntary union for life of a man and a woman increasingly wobbly. Once it is admitted that a marriage has broken down if even one spouse wants to end it, it has to be true to say 'You can always get a divorce' and even 'You may always be divorced whether you like it or not. Your only safeguard is your trust in your partner, just as it would be if you were cohabiting. The law may take an interest in your economic plight or the arrangements for your children, but it no longer underwrites your wish to think of yourself as decisively united to somebody else.'

Maybe it will be decided that it is no longer public policy to underwrite any such wish, but the continuing popularity of marriage emphasized in study after study suggests that permanent union continues to be widely wanted, and not only on behalf of the children. But also, even if inconsistently, public opinion wants the safety-valve of divorce to be available; so the problem is to provide the safety-valve without at the same time completely opening the floodgates. There is a process by which the unthinkable becomes first thinkable and then practicable, and the 'de-legalization of marriage' is an idea which has already been mooted. This would mean that the law would take no cognizance of whatever marriage ceremonies people chose to participate in: there would be no legal distinction between marriage and cohabitation, and therefore, in law, no marriage or divorce. 'The abdication of the State from any responsibility for determining whether a divorce should be granted'[8] would be a distinct first step in that direction, though this abdication seems to follow on smoothly once the breakdown principle is accepted.

Already complaints are being made that what the law provides is not monogamy but 'serial polygamy'. The law of divorce seems to move on inexorably beyond 'divorce with consent' to 'divorce by consent'. If it moves on again to divorce by unilateral demand,[9] the question needs to be seriously faced from what sort of bond divorce is being taken to set people free. To ask questions about the meaning of marriage is not to make inappropriate value judgements about human relationships, but to enquire about the goals of public policy and the most likely way to achieve or fail to achieve them.

THE CHURCH AND THE LAW

When Christians are asked for their opinion about divorce legislation they need to make it clear that their concern is not to fasten religious views upon everyone, still less to punish sinners, but to keep open the live option of a man and a woman taking each other, not just as partners, but as husband and wife. That is what they should keep in mind in commending or opposing changes. Not carping criticism but comprehension of the difficulties is what will deserve to be heeded.

Because church people in England took a part in getting 'breakdown' accepted as the basis for divorce rather than the matrimonial offence, there is no reason why they should have to welcome all subsequent developments. The idea of 'breakdown' has taken on an unfortunate life of its own, being used to mean not final shipwreck but self-justifying natural hazard. Hindsight tells us that when we risk opening floodgates we do open floodgates. When we try to build in safeguards those safeguards are almost bound to be swept away, for economic reasons if no other.

We cannot expect even the most logically worked out position to satisfy both liberals and rigorists: we may be obliged to make decisions between them. The argument that marriages can and sometimes do come to grief and that such failure is the most realistic ground of divorce leaves many decisions open about how the bond is to be severed and about what is to remain of the obligations the spouses undertook. There must be scope here for taking into account larger issues than the immediate wishes of estranged husbands and wives.

Christians may well urge that 'no fault' as a dogma, superseding the older straitjacket of the 'matrimonial offence', has gone far enough; and that the 'clean break' has already gone too far. It is not even realistic, let alone just, to assume that it ought to be possible

71

simply to untie the bond of marriage without fuss and leave the erstwhile spouses to face the world in independence of one another as if they had never been married. Of course compassionate people, including Christians, like the idea of a second chance and a fresh start; but giving priority to a new family, which is the practical effect of the 'clean break', brushes aside the meaning of the first marriage and takes little notice of natural justice. Advocates of the 'breakdown' principle need to remember that it has to remove a longstanding right, the right of an innocent spouse not to be divorced at all. This right cannot remain if breakdown is to take over from the matrimonial offence; but attempts are reasonably made to build in some protection. These attempts are now often decried as unrealistic and even undesirable, such a hold has the 'clean break' taken upon public opinion.

It is being argued that the right way to prevent economic hardship after divorce is not to encourage people to continue to feel responsible for their rejected spouses, but to discourage dependence even during marriage. But dependence is not only a matter of economic need, important though that is when a woman has given her youth to looking after the family. When two people have had even a few years to grow together they simply are not the two who fended for themselves humanly and emotionally before they were married. Not just a 'meal ticket' but a person who has become part of one's life is what is cut off by a decree of divorce, and the ready assumption that a clean break is best will not be much help in healing such a scar.

If Christian insights are to be brought to bear here, it is useless to expect talk about indissolubility or marriage as a sacrament to carry weight. Theological concern for what is good for human beings must be expressed in terms of social concern. The most hopeful sign is the emphasis increasingly laid upon conciliation when reconciliation will not avail. The recommendation that divorce should be understood as a process rather than as a clear-cut event, and that time should be taken to solve the problems of severing the bond, is an encouraging feature of current discussion.[10] There is an analogy here to the work of hospices in looking after patients whose illness is past cure. Marriages, like people, may die a 'good death' and leave sadness rather than bitterness behind. But nobody would want a hospice to deny the misery of terminal illness and preach a 'clean break' for the bereaved rather than mourning.

Nor would one think much of the hospice movement as a substitute for finding out how to prevent or cure cancer. Christians have the right to continue to insist that divorce is contrary to human happiness: not an unreasonable taboo but truly a social evil. Nor are they alone in maintaining this. Secular wisdom increasingly agrees, especially for the sake of the children who are the real victims when their parents decide to part.[11] It is defeatism, not approval, that allows the continuing slide into almost automatic divorces with no chance for anyone to take the part of the innocent casualties.

It is easier to be critical than to be constructive; but if Christian opinion is to count for anything Christians must try to offer some tentative practical suggestions, even if only to indicate what they believe to be important. The need is to build into the divorce law some recognition of the public interest in stable unions. To do this, if it could be done, would surely be more in line with public opinion than a legal withdrawal from the institution of marriage.

Would-be solutions offered by non-experts are apt to be soon knocked down, either by the experts or by hard facts. One may best be constructive by trying to make plain what we need. One tempting answer which we do not need is to try to show our concern for children by forbidding divorce to spouses with young families and allowing it much more easily to childless people. This would be unsatisfactory both in theory and in practice. In theory, it would amount to a denial that childless marriage is real marriage. In practice, it is easy to imagine the effects upon families. Unhappy motives would be introduced for having, or not having, children; and a child once there could become a focus of bitterness for the parent who wanted to be free.

Yet it is concern for families which has brought so many people to the conviction that divorce is a major evil of our times. Such concern must have weight in whatever is done about improving divorce laws. Long ago in the 1960s, Lord Devlin argued that what a divorce court is really doing is not dissolving some spiritual bond but licensing remarriage.[12] More than twenty years later it is increasingly clear that it is the greatly expanded right to abandon one marriage and form another which constitutes the social problem of divorce. The developing right to set up a new family and let society pick up the pieces is, to put it at its lowest, an inordinate expense for society. Would it be unreasonable to expect divorcing spouses to show, not only (too easily) that their marriage has failed, but also that to release them from it would not be too much against the public interest?

Of course such a 'breakdown plus' requirement would insert some uncertainty into the law: that is what it would be there for. The uncertainty need not be very great. Most divorces could go through quite easily and cheaply, just as most people do not have their luggage unpacked in the Customs. But the law could retain a right to have a say in the matter, without being obliged to pretend unrealistically that breakdown had not occurred. It could reasonably be deemed that marriages, as it were, firm up with time, so that early divorces would not need such expensive attention as later ones. Children's rights could take their proper place as part of the public interest, if their parents' right to claim divorce did not have to be so absolute. Conduct need not be considered as essentially irrelevant so that we have to watch helplessly while unscrupulous Casanovas take advantage of their own wrong. Under a law based simply on the failure of marriage, lovers can securely put on pressure for the bond to be broken, in the confidence that sooner or later on they must win. Would some sort of asymmetrical decree, refusing one spouse permission to switch resources to a new family, be an outrageously retrogressive idea, in certain hard cases where ready divorce offends against natural justice yet it cannot be denied that the marriage has broken down?

Maybe some hopeless unions would have to be kept in being; but maybe it would generally meet the case to impose a greater or less delay. The object of this approach to divorce would be to give the law a continuing point of entry at the very place where the public interest is indeed concerned, and where breakdown as sole criterion renders everyone but the spouses helpless. The necessary expense of keeping divorce judicial, not only administrative, would be the price paid for maintaining the concept of marriage itself.

– 9 –

Holy wedlock

Come, come, whoever or whatever you may be, come
Infidel, heathen, fireworshipper, idolater, come
Though you have broken your penitence a hundred times,
Ours is not the portal of despair and misery, come.

Mevlana, the founder of the Whirling Dervishes

PARTING OF WAYS?

Suppose that none of the arguments against radical reform of the divorce law prevails, and the law develops in such a way that marriage becomes practically indistinguishable from cohabitation. At what point ought Christians to say, 'This is too much: what the law calls marriage has moved too far away from the true meaning of marriage for us to be able to say that we are talking about the same institution'? And if that point is reached, what then?

It has been important to the Church to be able to recognize secular weddings as real weddings. The notice in register offices announcing that marriage is a lifelong union has meant a lot. If that notice effectively became a dead letter, it would be dishonest to pretend that this made no difference. If, in theory, marriage became a contract terminable by the simple action of one spouse, or if, in practice, the exceptions became so numerous as to swamp the norm, the law of the land would have failed to keep open, as it has more or less done so far, the option of entering into a decisively permanent union. There would be implications for Christian policies, concerning both first weddings and the problem of remarriage after divorce, but not quite the implications that some serious Christians assume.

It is too easy to jump to the conclusion that the time has come to insist that 'Christian marriage' is something special. It is being argued, in a way that seems obvious to many, that the blurring of the boundaries between the Church and the world, to which the Church of England is particularly prone, ought to stop: that people who owe allegiance to Christ and are prepared to commit themselves to obey his commands should make their vows in church, while the rest may do as they please and have their divorces if they must.

This recurrent belief in two kinds of marriage is a danger, not an answer. It matches the secular threat, to close the option of lifelong union, with a Church threat to close it to everyone except Christians. But there are not two kinds of marriage, the holy or the secular, made by the State or made by the Church. There is one kind, made by the couple in the sight of God. Many couples have wanted, more or less definitely, to recognize God's presence and ask for His blessing at this solemn time. Others have not wanted this, but have wanted just as truly to be married.

If the seriousness of register office marriage is weakened still further by changes in the divorce law, church people will have an increased responsibility for not denying the option of truly 'getting married' to their fellow human beings. The more dissatisfied Christians are with the legal framework provided by the civil authorities as a basis for human flourishing, the more need there is for the Church to play a part in supplying what the law of the land inadequately provides. Far from hankering after universal civil marriage followed by church ceremonies reserved for believers, Christian ministers who conduct weddings ought to look on themselves as welcoming people through a special door into a large room.

A plausible but dangerous suggestion is that at least the Church should be allowed to insist that two people both unbaptized can claim no right to be married in the name of the Trinity. The thought of what the attempt to put this principle into effect could do to baptism ought to be daunting. Whatever we may think is a good reason for wanting to be baptized or to have one's baby baptized, meeting legal conditions for a church wedding is a bad reason. There are plenty of arguments for and against a liberal baptism policy, but to superimpose a strict wedding policy upon the present disagreements would be to deter some of the most sincere, to let in some of the most superficial, and to introduce a disastrously false impression that the Church acting in God's name cares mainly for proper qualifications.[1]

WELCOME

Some heed must be taken of the heart-searchings which are going on about church weddings.[2] People can and do expect to be married in their parish church even when normally they never set foot there and even when they are not in any plain way believers. Some of the clergy find this ministry to the semi-detached particularly rewarding.[3] Others find it particularly frustrating. One can feel some sympathy for their discouragement at being made to feel that the church is being used and, worse, that God's name is being taken in vain, just to provide an old-world setting for a party. One must feel less sympathy for the attempts, often only too successful, that are made to freeze these enquirers out; or to use the 'pastoral opportunity' to lecture them and maybe the congregation as well about the evils of divorce.

It need be neither weak nor hypocritical, though it may be time-consuming, to take the risk of setting these anxieties aside as far as possible and offering God's grace and blessing with whole-hearted rejoicing. There need be no element of pretence here, and it is not for us to judge the element of waste. If the cup into which we are trying to pour something is too small, it will overflow; but all human vessels are too small. The Church is not 'going through the motions' of an empty rite, making people mouth what they simply do not mean. It is doing for them what they have asked, giving them the opportunity to take each other as husband and wife 'in the presence of God and in the face of this congregation'. To take each other as husband and wife is a humanly, indeed a legally, valid act, not a hollow show.

When people with a seemingly inadequate understanding of what they are about come and ask the Christian Church to adorn and beautify their wedding with a holy blessing, who are we to put difficulties in their way? The proper attitude for the churches to take up towards people getting married is appreciative rather than defensive. The Christian role is not so much to witness, negatively, to 'Christian standards' as to welcome, to celebrate in the fullest sense. In a different meaning of 'witness' though their role is precisely that: not to uphold marriage against possible foes, but to be present in God's name when two people marry each other.

When people want to solemnize their marriage in church, however inarticulate they may be about what it means to them, it smacks of meanness and possessiveness for Christians to try to ration God's blessing. Nor should church members belittle the extent to which an engaged couple may be looking, even unawares, for something 'spiritual' although they are too shy to show it; and the most extrovert people are often the shyest about religion. If encouragement and enthusiasm are what they find when they approach the Church about their deepest human concerns, they are far more likely to be able to recognize the grace and blessing of God when it is offered to them. It is not altogether easy for the clergy to comprehend that religion may be a kind of unmention-able subject in the way in which sex is supposed to have been in the nineteenth century. A wedding is an occasion both natural and happy when this taboo on piety is apt to weaken. Should it not be seized upon, not for instant evangelism but for building up less timid attitudes?

Even where the happy couple's frame of mind is impenetrably social, it can still be worth showing that Christians are capable of rejoicing with those who rejoice, without nagging about divorce or snatching greedily at 'pastoral opportunities'. Unless there is open scorn of what the Church stands for, it is more appropriate to think of the rain falling alike upon the just and the unjust than of pearls being cast before swine. Perhaps the young people are only conforming to please their parents? That in itself is not negligible. It is surely hard on the parents when this attempt to please is treated as wholly unworthy.

The damage done by an unwelcoming stance may spread through several generations, unrecognized by those responsible, who think that they have upheld Christian marriage. People who have been discouraged by the attitude of their clergy often do not argue: they simply go away, sometimes for ever. They will be polite to the vicar but let the world know what they think of his Christianity; and probably in due course bring up their children to assume 'The church is not for the likes of us'.

A church ceremony on the contrary gives a chance for families and friends to pray for the bride and bridegroom, and for the whole congregation, however worldly they may appear, at least to see that something significant is happening. This joining of two lives is humanly important in the way that birth and death are important. The sacred and the secular meet here whether those concerned are pious or impious. This is what the Church is claiming when it is present in God's name at a wedding.

Can we value the Christian wedding service so highly without belittling the alternative? We offer marriage in church as a way of entering into a real and permanent union; and the more we honour people's integrity, the more we understand that a church wedding means a lot to them. So a contrast, whether we like it or not, is set up by the valued solemnity of our service, with the other way of getting married which simply makes two people husband and wife without giving them the chance to make such serious vows. So are we landed after all with two kinds of marriage, the perishable kind made in register offices and the imperishable kind which A. P. Herbert long ago called 'holy deadlock'? Voltaire said that the best is the enemy of the good. Much as Christians may want to allow and even insist that secular marriage is true marriage, how can they deny that a wedding in church ties the knot better after all?

If in register offices there comes to be less and less effective emphasis on permanence, so that people who believe in lifelong marriage are driven to rely increasingly on the permanence of vows made in church, it will come to look more and more as if a church wedding ties a different kind of knot and does not just tie the same kind of knot in a preferred way. This is the moment to be particularly careful not to slip into the idea that all this is a matter of religious belief. Far from beginning now to have doubts about a liberal policy over marriage in church because it blurs the distinction between believer and unbeliever, one could almost say that such a policy is desirable partly for that very reason. If we are forced reluctantly to draw lines between kinds of marriage, at least we need not draw the line between 'Christian marriage' and the supposedly wobbly unions of everyone else.

WITNESS

The principle of welcoming practically all comers can evidently not be applied as it stands to people who have been married before and divorced. Because we believe that marriage is a way of joining a man and a woman in a lifelong union, we cannot simply forget about permanence or treat it as an unattainable ideal the moment it comes under pressure.

Ever a limited admission that marriage in church is more 'special' than register office weddings forbids us to spoil this specialness by not honouring it. The fact that we encourage people to come to church to be married, because we believe that what we have to offer them is an especially appropriate way of giving each other their consent, forbids us to undermine all this by seeming to make light of the permanence they undertake.

It is no wonder that rigorism is still so strong. Rigorists refuse to complicate the problem of remarriage after divorce. They hold to the assumption that for people who have been properly married the first time, any thoughts of entering into a second union while the first spouse is still alive must be out of the question. Christian mercy comes in with the concession that plenty of spouses are not married in a Christian sense at all. Many loyal church people hope that a rigorist stance, mitigated by concessions for the uncommitted, will uphold the values we need but still allow us to show a wide tolerance, at least to all the numbers of divorced people more or less outside the Christian fold.

Neither the strictness nor the tolerance is realistic. On the one hand it is no use to shut one's eyes to the possibility of truly married people coming to grief. It is only too clear that even the most solemn vows give no guarantee against matrimonial disaster. We may hope that there will be fewer casualties when people enter into marriage with serious intent, but there will be some casualties even among practising Christians, and these may be among the most miserable. It would seem to be a long way from the teaching of Christ to be sure that they can never make a fresh start.

On the other hand the tenacious notion of the double standard is hindrance rather than help.[4] If our understanding of marriage is rightly founded on the biblical teaching about the 'one-flesh union' of a man and a woman, and is no special preserve of believers, then the 'hard sayings' about divorce which we also take to go back to the Lord are likewise not restricted to Christians. It is patronizing to suggest that most of our contemporaries, who are perhaps 'invincibly ignorant', are free to do as they please, while we faithful few are obliged to obey God's commands. The present arrangements for getting married, which blur the distinction between believer and unbeliever, are beneficial partly for the very reason that they make any such double standard almost impossible to apply.

What can the Christian Church do for people who ask for mercy and a new beginning? What we are aiming at is an interpretation of marriage as *characteristically* permanent which still makes some allowance for casualties, including Christian casualties. In trying to achieve this we have not much room for manoeuvre. We must not substitute legalism for the grace of God; nor instead dilute the principles we are supposed to stand for, affirming that marriage is for life but acting as if it were not.

The Church of England has been trying to deal with this problem for many years and has seemed to be on the brink of arriving at a fairly reasonable way of handling it. There seems to be a convergence of opinion that it is not right, either in theory or in practice, to treat divorced and remarried people as literally 'living in sin'. In other words, our best understanding of the teaching of Christ, taken as a whole, is that putting asunder is wrong rather than impossible. The question of how vows can ever be remitted remains more recalcitrant,[5] but it is fair to say that a good deal of agreement has been reached on the theology of marriage. The intractable difficulty of the whole divorce problem is now concentrated upon how the mercy Christians want to show is compatible with their vocation to witness to a better way of doing things.

The agreement which was all but reached was that it may be possible for a second marriage to be the best outcome in the circumstances and even, we may believe, the will of God for the people concerned. Granted that such a new start can be made, it is bound to have the weight of the past hanging upon it, and will need all the help and blessing it can have. To say 'Go away and get married as best you can and then we will recognize you as husband and wife' seems hardly honest, let alone generous. That is the strength of the argument for allowing people to make their new promises in church. There is the risk of offence and scandal either way. What successive Church commissions emphasized, though compassionate liberals are apt to forget, is that whatever is done should be plainly seen to be a positive and special act of mercy on behalf of the whole Church, not a freelance attempt to minister to individuals without looking at the whole picture.

So far began to seem so good. But this emerging common mind, trying to comprehend both clarity and compassion, sank in a morass of legalism.[6] It was defeated by the difficulty of laying down guidelines for clergy who had actually to decide who could be remarried in church and who could not. The notion of 'safeguards' took a strong hold, and safeguards seemed to have more to do, not with *how* remarriages could be solemnized responsibly, but with *whose* remarriages would be in order.

So we are left with individuals trying to do their best, and the main point has been lost, that any remarriage which is not merely permissive must be a sort of loosing and binding in the name of Christ. It is no wonder that 'services of blessing' for divorced people, after register office remarriages, have found so much favour lately as the best way to show mercy and maintain loyalty both at once. Perhaps at present this is the only practical answer, and it is probably better than no answer at all; but the idea of a blessing as a second-best is deeply flawed. If we can bless these people's undertaking, do we or do we not believe that what they are doing is in accordance with God's will? What do we suppose that they are doing, if it is not promising each other to be faithful for the rest of their lives? So do we after all send them away to make their promises and not quite commit ourselves about whether they are really married in the sight of God?

The rationale of all this is that Christian witness shall be preserved. Something will have been said about a second marriage not being simply a matter of course. As usual, even more depends upon the sensitivity with which a service is conducted than the exact form it takes. Quite illogical ways of coping with situations can turn out to work very well and come to mean a lot to people. 'Services of blessing' may be a blessing. But if they are used for the sake of 'witness' it ought always to be asked to what exactly they are witnessing. A small mean service may be more like a punishment than a sign of the grace of God. A large and grand service, just like a wedding except for the absence of vows, may be a witness to indecision and confusion of mind, even to hypocrisy. It may be as hurtful to anybody who still minds about the first marriage as a 'proper

81

wedding' would have been. It would be much better, if the Church really is able to countenance remarriages of divorced people, if it could devise a way of first plainly setting them free to remarry and then allowing them solemnly to take on their new obligations 'in the sight of God' with priest and congregation as witnesses.

When one thinks of some of the bitter disputes going on in the Church at present, mostly between traditionalists and radicals, the comparative convergence of opinion about marriage and divorce gives a good deal of reason for optimism. It has to be admitted that this optimism is reduced by current doubts about what is going to happen to marriage in our society. If on the one hand the sheer number of divorces continues to increase, and on the other hand the law of the land moves in the direction it quite likely may, the Church's room for manoeuvre will be further reduced. It has so far been the basis of Christian attempts to give people second chances that disastrous marriages could indeed be looked on as casualties, impairing but not destroying the characteristic permanence of marriage as understood by the Church, by public opinion, and by the law of the land. There was a lot of scope for mercy, because it was based on so much agreement about its terms of reference. If people are going to be able to say realistically 'You can always get a divorce', the Church will have to be even more careful than it has been so far not to give them reason to add 'and of course you can have a second wedding just as good as the first'.

The Church of England might find itself forced into becoming not only more rigorist but more legalist. If it were no longer in a position to concentrate upon grace and let the civil authorities take care of legality, it might need to formulate more precisely laws of its own about the marriage bond, and this would be both saddening and confusing. Before we find ourselves in a position where only Church courts instead of individual and generally informal pastoral care will meet our problems, it is urgent that we should consolidate the common mind we partly have about the theory and practice of what goes by the name of 'marriage discipline'.

I tried to give an analysis some years ago[7] of how matters stood in the Church, an analysis which unfortunately has been partly fulfilled and seems worth repeating. Whatever the Church decides it ought to say, it is likely to be misunderstood. If it is rigorist, it will be thought unforgiving. If it is liberal, it will be thought to abandon Christ's teaching. If it tries to explain a more subtle view, it will be thought to be liberal or rigorist. If it sets up practical safeguards there will be pressure to remove them. All that can be said is that the risks are great on all sides, so that the only thing to do is what ought to be done anyway, consider what is right and then consider how best to explain it. Certainly if the Church does not come to some definite decision it will have the worst of both worlds. Its present policy loyally put into effect is not escaping, and I believe cannot escape, the taint of legalism; and unless it can be established afresh it will not continue to be loyally put into effect. There will be more dissentients who feel obliged to go ahead with remarriage in church without tarrying for any, without the corporate backing which alone can make such remarriage theologically justifiable. Human pity is a poor substitute for the mercy of God offered by the Church speaking in his name. Meanwhile the world will lose interest in mercy and pity and will go its own way, looking for secular blessings and claiming rights. So in the end it could lose by default one of the greatest of all the secular blessings in God's creation, the human institution of faithful monogamous marriage in which total trust is built up over a number of years into a bond experienced as unbreakable.

– 10 –

Parents and children

Wisdom doth live with children round her knees . . .
William Wordsworth, Sonnet: 'I grieved for Buonaparté'

PRIORITIES

When the union between husband and wife is given due importance for its own sake, there begins to be an opposite risk of forgetting the biological purpose of marriage. When all the emphasis is on 'personal relationships' there may develop a kind of romantic sentimentality which isolates couples from their context in families. This is a way to lose touch, not only with the biblical tradition, but with realism about men and women as we find them. One reason why the 'pairbond' is a useful notion, in some ways even more useful than relationship, is that while allowing plenty of scope for love and loyalty it is also a concept used in the study of animal behaviour. It roots human beings in their biological context, as creatures who characteristically unite with one another in twos in order to reproduce themselves and to bring up their offspring.

Both emphases are needed, relationship and fruitfulness. It is embarrassing for a Christian moralist to realize how distorted Christian teaching has been here, how procreation has been over-emphasized, how slowly the Christian Churches have come to recognize that sexuality has more than reproductive value. One must deplore the imbalance in the Christian tradition which gave no value to physical pleasure and grudging approval to human affections, but expected human beings obediently to set about peopling the earth in a spirit of detached duty. The earth is over-peopled now and the most ardent opponent of contraception does not really suppose that the production of babies is the sole justification for marriage, still less that the more babies people have the better.

Yet new life is still wonderful and people are still enthralled to become parents. The practice of birth control which separates sexual union from fertility and allows the avoidance or postpone-

84

ment of conception, has curiously enough had the effect of bringing offspring into prominence again as a primary purpose of marriage. It happens often now that people live together as unmarried partners until they decide to start a family. When they are about to become parents they make their union official. This is not a 'shotgun wedding'. They may have intended it, or anyway hoped for it, all along. They would be deeply hurt if instead of rejoicing with them their friends treated their marriage as a *faute de mieux*. They have made the choice to allow procreation to be the consequence of their lovemaking, whereas for previous generations offspring simply had to be accepted.

In the contrary situation when people are married and the marriage proves infertile, the separation of sexual union from the hope of a family is involuntary and maybe grievous. Tantalizing chances can now be offered of achieving parenthood after all, real parenthood though technically brought about. Should moralists be anxious? 'Test-tube babies' may find it as hard to win their way as birth control has. Birth control artificially separates sexual relationship from procreation, though with authentic hope of eventually enhancing both rather than undermining them. The new techniques of fertilization make the separation the other way round and try to achieve offspring apart from sexual union; yet still for the sake of restoring the twofold character of marriage, so that the unity of two people shall bring another generation into existence. The intervention of applied science is not a matter of heartlessly manufacturing babies. Test tubes are not 'natural' but need not therefore be alien. Human technology can build bridges as well as barriers.

Of course technology can be a mixed blessing. When contraception divorces sexual pleasure not only from fertility but from fidelity, when artificial insemination offers the 'right to have a child' even without a father, one can understand why moralists worry about slippery slopes. But traditional behaviour is stronger and more deeply ingrained in human nature than many people hope or fear. Men and women want to find partners who will stay with them through thick and thin. They seldom want to give priority for long to the simple pursuit of pleasure. When they fall in love they are apt to want their love to bear fruit, to confer existence upon new human creatures who will be both like and unlike their parents. There is a powerful and honourable wish to share with a growing generation whatever one has found good in this life.

The false emphases which have beset Christian thinking about sex and marriage are partly a matter of cutting off discussion too quickly so that only half the story is told. Marriage is for continuing the race; marriage is for uniting a man and a woman: both these are true. The way to reconcile them is not to decide which shall have priority, nor to make a kind of half-and-half compromise, but to go for a walk with Alice in the looking-glass country, where you miss the destination you aim at and find it when you head the other way. To bring up children, what is needed is secure and balanced adults. To make a good marriage, a man and a woman need to have something to attend to outside their two selves.

There seems to be a tendency in human life which might be called the principle of the glorified by-product. There are certain human goals which notoriously elude us, like the crock of gold at the rainbow's end, when we aim at them directly. The most conspicuous of these are happiness and originality. When people attempt to determine priorities among the 'causes for which Matrimony was ordained' they encounter a similar phenomenon. Whatever we fix upon as the primary purpose of marriage has a way of turning out to be quite unsatisfactory when it is given priority over everything else.

For centuries procreation was overemphasized and now love has been discovered or re-discovered as the essence of marriage, which is excellent unless it becomes self-enclosed. The kind of love between a man and a woman, married or not, which shuts out everyone but the beloved is likely to have little to offer to the beloved but constraint and claustrophobia. Romance cannot really be a complete vocation. So procreation comes into its own again as a matter of duty, to rescue the couple from selfishness. But parenthood in turn is not an end in itself. What is the point of having children, if the point will then be that they shall have children of their own, and so on indefinitely?

Parenthood is no more suitable than romance to be made into a vocation: indeed less suitable, because unlike romance it is temporary in its very nature. As an end in itself, the vocation of parenthood has failure built into it, because when it is achieved and the children have grown out of dependence, the parents who have lived for parenthood will have nothing left to live for. A wife who has not really noticed that she has been neglecting her husband, because her devotion was not to a career but to the family, can find herself retired before retiring age, longing to become a granny and tempted to put pressure on her daughters and sons so that she may continue to exercise the only skills she has fully developed.

Dedicated motherhood sometimes puts a strain on everybody, including the children. To be somebody's vocation in life, the *raison d'être* whether of parent or of paramour, is not the sort of priority that really satisfies human beings. A son and heir who is the apple of his parent's eye is less to be envied than children who grow up knowing that their mother and father put each other first. It begins to look as if we are trapped in a circle: we must both subordinate children to parents and parents to children. The 'principle of the glorified by-product' allows us happily to do just that.[1]

Instead of a hierarchy of 'ends of marriage' to be put in order there can develop, less self-consciously, a kind of pattern of rewards. The love between a man and a woman, instead of remaining self-enclosed, bears fruit in their offspring, who thrive best as part of a larger love. To grow up looking forward to maturity, knowing what it is for people to matter to each other, is better than to grow up as a temporary mini-god. The strenuous exercise of raising a family is one way of bringing down to earth the vague aspirations of a pair of lovers; and, if all goes well, of filling in their unformed hopes with reality. Satisfying relationships, between men and women and between the generations, turn out to be a harvest to be reaped, not a kind of examination to be passed.[2] The best way to reap this harvest in the end is not to be keep pulling it up by the roots to see whether it is growing, but to get on hopefully with the business in hand. Time is on our side when we let fulfilment steal up on us at its own pace, rather than fretting over compulsory goals.

MUST PRIORITIES BE TYRANTS?

Is this hope of achieving good relationships 'just an ideal'? Of course it is, but not if 'an ideal' means merely an extra, less definite, goal to be kept in mind, seldom achieved but not making us feel too guilty when we fail. If it is part of the meaning of ideals to be unrealistic, then rewarding family life does not have to be called an ideal. There is nothing impracticable about it. Criticism lies in quite another direction. The fruition of the family is indeed 'ideal' in being the attainment of what many people deeply want, and so it cannot be harmlessly unimportant. The promise of available happiness cannot help setting up a hurtful contrast between success and failure. The thoughtless unkindness of the couple to the single, of the fertile to the childless and of the easy-going to the tangled is pervasive and profoundly hurtful.

When ideals become stereotypes, there are large possibilities of the cruelty which consists of making people who are unable or unwilling to fit the stereotypes feel guilty. Christians have not a very good record here. Christianity is supposed to be able to deal with guilt, but is sometimes capable of exacerbating it. The 'Christian family' makes plenty of people feel excluded, not strengthened.

The working wife feels selfish for putting her career before her home; and, if it is a job rather than a career, for being materialist when maybe she is just gregarious. Meantime the housewife blames herself for stagnating among the toys and the dishes. People who try to combine children and a job have to add to inevitable tiredness a niggling guilt for not managing both perfectly, so becoming still more tired. Fathers are being subjected nowadays to this two-sided battery. Did they attend the birth? Do they change nappies? Do they support their families? Are they gentle? Are they strong? Even grandparents may have an awkward path to tread between interference and aloofness. Divorced people have stigma as well as shipwreck to contend with. Single parents, whether widowed or divorced, have no secure niche in society. Men and women who find themselves outside family life because they are homosexual are despised even though not prosecuted. Some of these people are coping outstandingly well in difficult circumstances; some are and feel themselves to be in a mess.

When the blame for all these discontents is put upon the ideal of the happy family, it is no wonder that hopeful people become anxious whether perhaps they ought to be less hopeful, for fear of smugness on the one hand or of discouragement on the other. So they play down the good they have, rather than risk being unkind to other people or incurring their envy. That is how excellent possibilities may go by default to the impoverishment of everyone.

What is most needful is to recognize reciprocally the possible and actual glory of variegated kinds of achievement, so as to have less need to be either envious or patronizing towards one another. It is high time that people stopped imagining that their own well-trodden ways of living are the norm and that everyone else must be outlandish. Married lives and single lives, the strains of bringing up children, the unity of a husband and wife who have no children, the attainment of ambition, the harder attainment of overcoming disappointment, all have their own integrity. The world could be more of a caucus race than people allow it to be: *'Everybody* has won (or at least a great many people have), and *all* must have prizes', not just consoling pats on the back.

When a harvest is reaped, gratitude is in order. That sounds plain enough: who would want to crab it? Unfortunately one person's happy gratitude may sound like gloating, and demand a good deal of other people in patience and magnanimity. Surprisingly often, for someone without any particular harvest at the moment, there seems to be hardly any room for manoeuvre between sourness and supererogatory goodness. The neutral ground where people are neither resentful nor generous is disconcertingly narrow. It is seldom perfectly all right to be just good enough. The 'saving grace', literally, is that the extra kindness we need can itself be a by-product. When people set themselves, which they can do as a beginning, to be 'good enough' to one another, the 'enough' has a way of moving on as they proceed, towards something more positive than they first supposed. Not to be unkind edges its way into being kind.

An important lesson in generosity which is less elementary than it looks is to enter into somebody else's happiness when dreams come true. Contrariwise, one way of getting the worst of all worlds, of losing sight of glory without overcoming bitterness, is to belittle what we can see for ourselves to be good, whether in envy of other people's blessings or modesty about our own. It is deeply sad to try to prevent feelings of jealousy from getting the upper hand by complaining of the children's sticky fingers, and losing touch with their enchanting affection. To understand that what we are delighting in is a by-product rather than an achievement is more comfortable for everybody, because possessiveness, and with it credit and blame, can be left out of account. People can rejoice in glory wherever they become aware of it, without either gloating over success or using it as a stick to beat other people.

IMAGE OF CREATION

So it is right to be grateful for the possible glory of married love, as a creative love which characteristically gives birth and nurture to new lives. 'Characteristically' is the keyword. There is no need to imagine presumptuously that this is either the whole story about marriage or the only real hope of human fulfilment: yet people who have found family life good may be encouraged to celebrate it, in all humility. If they are Christians they may reasonably believe that what they have found is in accord with God's purposes. Such a conviction is more likely to prove attractive when the people who hold it are spontaneously in good heart, than 'Christian family life' dutifully preached as a kind of nasty medicine against social evils.

It means something definite, not tautologous, to say that married love can be a creative love. It is worth taking a look at the notion of 'pro-creation' to see what Christian sustenance can be drawn out of it. Parenthood, like marriage, may be able to offer a two-way illumination, interpreting the Christian faith and in turn being interpreted by it.[3]

We say that people are made in the image of God and this can have many meanings. One meaning is that we are like our Maker in being creators. Human beings truly take part in shaping the world they live in: with clumsiness or care, skill or even genius. The most ordinary and yet the most important kind of creation delegated to humankind is the begetting, bearing and bringing up of new people. Of course we 'play God'. If we are His children it is our proper role to do just that. We are pleased for our children to play at being like us. Their play, and ours, is a real and significant part of growing up.

Children play with dolls and this is practice for maturity. Sometimes they invent dream companions. Dolls and dreams have a kind of reality projected on to them; whereas offspring are not made-up but made. A baby is what dolls and dreams pretend to be, a new person entering the world, whether loved or repudiated, whatever anyone happens to feel: with legal rights already and a particular personality beginning to develop, entirely vulnerable but not entirely malleable. Babies are not little slot-machines to respond with smiles instead of cries when one presses the right button. They have minds of their own. It does not take much imagination to be awestruck at the idea that a man and a woman, oneself maybe, have had the power to bring a new human being into the world and in a small way, or even in a large way, to change the course of history. Such power is literally God-like.

To attend to the autonomy of children is a way of correcting false pictures both of God's authority and of what it means to be a human parent. To create or to procreate is not an exercise in omnipotence but in standing back from omnipotence. It has been reiterated to the point of platitude that the object of it all is the nurturing of free mature people. Looking at real children can bring the platitude to life. Spirit and sparkle are more tiring but far more rewarding than meek docility. Why should we suppose that our heavenly Father is an over-protective parent who values nothing but obedience?

Human beings have wanted progeny for all sorts of reasons, conscious and unconscious: someone to love, support in old age, the continuance of a family line, duty or simple force of habit.

> This were to be new made when thou art old,
> And see thy blood warm when thou feel'st it cold

was a clinching reason for Shakespeare.[4] Children have been treated with neglect, devotion, sentimentality, harshness, matter-of-fact affection and various mixtures of these. It would be needless cynicism to refuse to look behind all this medley of selfishness and unselfishness for an authentic creative impulse, both ordinary and remarkable.

It is a fact about human marital love at its most secure that it tends not to remain self-enclosed but to complete itself in the love of offspring.[5] It is not a far-fetched piece of theology for Christians to see in this an image illuminating the secure and self-sufficient, but not self-enclosed, glory of the Holy Trinity. We have been taught that Father, Son and Holy Spirit do not need human creatures but rejoice to create us out of overflowing love: we might say as a by-product of eternal glory. As Thomas Traherne put it:

This is very strange that GOD should Want. For in Him is the Fulness of all Blessedness: He overfloweth Eternally. His Wants are as Glorious as infinit . . . He Wanted Angels and Men, Images, Companions. And these He had from all Eternitie.[6]

COMPARE AND CONTRAST

Finding and using analogies without being misled by them is a matter of balancing one with another. It is strange, when we have the image of 'Father' upon such high authority, that Christians have been so shy to take that comparison seriously, and have chosen to concentrate an excessively literal-minded attention upon God the Creator fashioning us like pots out of clay, rather than upon God our heavenly Father giving us life like a parent. The creation stories in Genesis emphasize God's delight in His handiwork, but unless they are balanced by other images they leave an impression of ready-made creatures, perfect all at once except for sin. There is a lot more to be said, not only by Darwin, to fill in the picture of the struggling untidy gradual development of mature human beings who will 'take after' their heavenly Father not least in being capable of standing on their own feet.

'Two-way illumination' is almost put into reverse here as people proceed to think of procreation too as if it were a kind of fashioning. Parents suppose that they can make their children, and when they find they cannot they blame either themselves or the recalcitrance of the raw material. Family life in its reality is apt to be somewhat different from what people have imagined, less like artistic creation and a good deal more like chaos.

Bringing up a family is not at all like being a sculptor moulding clay or chipping away at a block of stone that stays still to be worked upon. It is not much like being a gardener in a well-kept garden, with time to make plans and carry them out deliberately, to consider the soil and the weather, to keep off pests and prune at the proper time of year. It is more like an energetic dance than a quiet communing with nature: more like a game of tennis than a game of chess.

Someone who hopes to be a parent one day may have a picture of a way of going about it, which oddly enough existing parents generally seem not to achieve, in which one would do everything that was needed step by step, answer questions reasonably without embarrassment, mould opinions without brainwashing, build up a

91

reliable character rather like one's own ideal self and gradually introduce this delightful little person to the outer world. It turns out instead that the outer world is there from the start, that each stage comes and goes more quickly than one could have guessed, and that all the while the children take part in their own upbringing to such an extent that it becomes a joint enterprise.

Of course Christian parents do make use of the image of the Fatherhood of God, but sometimes in restricted ways. We assume too easily that He is the sort of parent who wants children to be all alike, docile and obedient rather than enterprising. Pious people think a lot about the pity God has for His sinful children, His acceptance of them with all their faults, His mercy on their backsliding. It would be less enervating to emphasize instead His giving us room to grow, His letting us take risks, His delight in our variety; even His amusement at our serious efforts to grow up.

'Acceptance' is important but often it is shrunk to acceptance of what we cannot like. But parents accept their children more thoroughly than this reluctant tolerance. They enjoy their different capabilities, and find that bringing them up is as much getting to know them as moulding them. It is not much good trying to make a reserved child demonstrative, but King Lear, if he had been more father than king, could have respected Cordelia's integrity, in which case we should have had no play. It is as cruel the other way round to try to make a naturally emotional child have a stiff upper lip, but one can encourage the direction of all this sensitivity towards other people.

Meantime one may find out the hard way about oneself, that in the pressure of family life when one's pride is so much involved one is not after all the calm steady person that it was easy to plan to be. At this point it is simply depressing to call conventionally upon the grace of God as a power always there to help if only people are humbly religious enough to ask. If parents were quietly capable they would find the time to pray to God to give them grace to be quietly capable. Meanwhile religious faith is all a matter of contrasting rather than comparing: 'How patient God is! How impatient we are!' But since God's patience is itself an invisible matter of faith it becomes one more item to believe, a hindrance rather than a help.

It is more sustaining to dare to make presumptuous comparisons, indeed to 'play God'. Christians call God 'Father' according to the teaching of Christ the Son. Calling God 'Father' is not just a kind of extra compliment to be paid to a remote God who sits on high and watches with benign tolerance: it is part and parcel of belief in a God who enters into the ordinary pressures of human life. So if we project not only parental love, but human experiences of the everyday struggles love demands, on to the God we worship, we do it on authority. It is not outrageous to affirm that within the Holy Trinity there is the experience of hardly having time for meals; the experience of having one's own family misunderstand what one is about; the experience of not being able to use human gifts to the full; even the experience of how infuriating people's wrong-headedness can be. The Lord is acquainted not only with temptation but with inconvenience and disorder. The achievement of an organized calm is not the only way of drawing near to God. 'Peace and quiet' must be something that people who follow Christ can either manage without or find in the middle of chaos.

IMAGE OF GRACE

If parents attempt a 'God's eye view' of what it means to be in charge of beloved and sometimes awkward children, they can see for themselves what kind of thing that grace is which they need so badly. They can fill in their idea of the love of God, as a parent's love: taking the child's part, unearned but not uncritical, beyond reason, merciful and demanding. So not only can they have more confidence in themselves as parents: they can be do-it-yourself theologians. All sorts of problematical Christian beliefs can come to life and have light shed upon them by human experience of family life.

Christianity is supposed to be about having faith: does this mean plumping irrationally for incredible certainties? Christianity requires believers to give things up: does this mean adopting a negative attitude to human life? The heart of Christianity is forgiveness: does this mean that Christians are supposed to be soft and unrealistic? Humanly speaking, believers are easily forced on to the defensive by questions like these. If one dares briefly to put oneself in the place of God the Father there is a chance of having a glimpse of what faith is and is not.

Suppose a grown-up has to take a splinter out of a child's finger. It would be a lie to say confidently 'It won't hurt'. People who rashly make that kind of affirmation are great destroyers of faith. What we do know is that there is a better chance of its not hurting if the child can somehow find the trust to keep still and not wriggle. We are not asking for a 'blind' faith. On the contrary, in this case it happens that it is lack of faith which is blind. The reasonable faith is swamped by the immediate stress. The analogy, of course, is limited. It does not help to explain how one is to come by this reasonable faith in the first place. Trusting God often seems less like trusting a Father we know than trusting that a strange frightening situation will be all right after all, because people we already trust tell us so. What the analogy does illustrate is the understandable wobbliness of faith: how it is all at once an almost impossible thing to ask, a necessary thing to ask and, once it can be looked at in retrospect, a small thing to ask.

Is the Christian religion full of negative renunciations? There are plenty of opportunities in family life for understanding that one good reason for giving things up may be, not that they are in any way bad but that they are spoilt by grabbing. Parents have to say to children 'Let go—or the toy will break': more often than 'Put away that useless rubbish'. They have to say 'Stop whining about the ice cream you cannot have', not because giving it up is better than having it, but because if people go on complaining neither they nor anyone else will be happy. They have to say 'Calm down, relax, make a happy face', not because what children want is unimportant but because like all human beings they rush into blind alleys. Grown-up people do not have to be scornful about children's tempers although sometimes they can stand back enough to see the funny side. Maybe adult rages sometimes have a comic rather than an evil aspect in the eyes of the heavenly Father. Christian morality, of course, cannot be reduced to these unheroic and juvenile concerns; but there is a good deal in the Gospel to suggest that 'becoming as little children' might include taking ourselves less solemnly.

Even Christian forgiveness can be illuminated by looking at childish quarrels. Often it is impossible to find out whose fault the trouble was. Each side is full of genuinely righteous indignation and there is an impasse unless somebody says 'Let's make it up'. In adult life this is deemed to put one hopelessly in the wrong, which makes it more difficult to understand that Christ did just that. Whatever the doctrine of the Atonement means, not standing on rights is a major part of it. When two children are quarrelling there is a chance for them to see how this works in practice: that no good will come unless somebody is prepared to be magnanimous. It is even more plain that when an adult is at odds with a child who has perhaps got into such a state as to be unable to say 'sorry', it can be godlike not weak to make the first move. Being sorry is apt to be quite easy when one has been treated with generosity. In any case this is surely a saner notion of people's ordinary sins: not some sort of impersonal contamination, but behaving impossibly and being in disgrace like a child.

If some of these examples seem a matter of mind-boggling triviality, this too makes a theological point. Belief that God entered into human life requires us to take seriously the narrow limitations that human life imposes. Theologians have a name for this: 'the scandal of particularity'. It must be either scandalous or awe-inspiring to believe that we are to worship as God a man who had a certain height and colouring, who needed to learn all his human knowledge from other people and from experience, who could carry out only a few purposes and meet only a few of his contemporaries, who would be tired at the end of every day and need sleep. The classic statement of the 'scandal of particularity' is: 'When thou tookest upon thee to deliver man: thou didst not abhor the Virgin's womb'. This is not an insult to womankind or to the mother of the Lord, but a reminder that becoming a human being means starting from very small and circumscribed beginnings.

There is a 'scandal of particularity', which can be a kind of image of the human life of the Lord, in families with young children. Parents find that what most matters to them is enmeshed in such triviality that it is a solecism to bring it into civilized conversation. The shrinking of intelligence to the scale of beloved but immature minds, the overwhelming importance of such concerns as feeds and nappies, the small tales to be told of milestones reached and long new words learnt, the impossibility of breaking out of these narrow boundaries without neglecting some duty: all this can give offence, or it can give a picture of the meaning of love.

At least it needs to be remembered that the triviality and limitation are not the whole story. The object of the whole exercise is nothing less than than the hope that the little people who are now immature may 'all attain', as the Epistle to the Ephesians puts it, 'to a perfect man', to which Christians will add, 'to the measure of the stature of the fulness of Christ'.[7]

– 11 –

Roles

Oh I must feel your brain prompt mine,
Your heart anticipate my heart . . .

Robert Browning, 'By the Fireside'

WIVES AND MOTHERS

It would hardly be possible to write convincingly about marriage today without attempting to sort out the newly insistent questions about the roles of women and men. Must we think of the differences, not only between 'male' and 'female', but between 'masculine' and 'feminine', as simply built into human life? What control, moral and practical, do we have over these differences?

The last chapter had a good deal to say about parents: but it would generally be realistic instead of 'parents' to read 'mothers'. It is still, quite naturally, women who have most to do with looking after families. It remains characteristic of women, whatever else they hope for as well, to want to bear children and to care for them. It is unlikely that this strong and sometimes desperate wish is all a matter of conditioning. It seems as powerful in girls who have been brought up to have careers as in girls whose upbringing has been directed towards domesticity. The longing for children catches up with feminists and traditionalists alike. It is even capable of being combined with a dislike of men. The fact that women become mothers is the abiding reason for their persistent vulnerability. The notion of 'equal opportunity' is an elusive one, whatever we think ought to be done about this.

What tends to be done about it is the adoption and defence of opposing stereotypes. Women in the Western world have of course come a long way and are nowadays deemed to have rights that their grandmothers hardly dreamt of, but the right which is slowest to be granted is the right to be variegated people, not simply 'women'. It is thought that they can be made happy as women, whether by establishing them securely as mothers or by releasing them from this necessity; or by adopting two stereotypes instead of one as if this

96

were a great step forward, so that some of the female sex can stay traditional and others can be liberated. So today women are apt to be allowed one great choice, which does not confront their husbands in such a stark form. Not all men can have their hopes of parenthood fulfilled, any more than all women can; but when men become fathers they are not expected to turn their backs on most of the rest of their human aspirations.

The most humane of today's feminists[1] are not trying to set women free from family life. They are talking about the choices of women rather than about their rights. To be allowed to beat biology by having no children at all is not much comfort to a woman who wants what most human beings want, to have the best of both worlds. Neither idealizing her as an Earth Mother nor lecturing her as a pupil who 'could do better' is going to help, though both these attempts to solve the problem are going on concurrently. The inspiring role of homekeeper and mother *is* an inspiring role and to many people an interesting and absorbing way of life, but it is no more inspiring and interesting to every woman than any one kind of responsible job appeals to every man.

Women who experience their lives as a series of chores are exhorted not to complain because every worthwhile occupation has its drudgery. They are accused, and what is worse they accuse themselves, of being ungrateful for their blessings and neglectful of the work they voluntarily took on. Many of them could not possibly have guessed before they found themselves immersed in family life what the fatigue and isolation of their allotted role would really amount to. Just because so many of them find it indeed worth while, to impose in the name of Motherhood upon their good nature and dedication is still an imposition.

A great deal can be done to improve many women's lives once it is accepted that alleviation of some of the pressures can be a more satisfying answer than setting women free from their complicated aspirations. All-day crèches taking children off their mothers' hands are a matter of family needs, not of making women happy. Part-time work, and better still job-sharing, deserve unpatronizing encouragement. More playgroups and nursery schools would be good for children, not just convenient for their mothers. It would help a good deal if people stopped supposing that only a full-scale vocation could justify a woman for wishing to occupy herself outside her home. Women frequently want to take ordinary humdrum paid jobs for all kinds of reasons, not the least of which can be that they would be bored and lonely with no grown-up company all day. Discontent is a poor sort of sacrifice to make, even lovingly, to one's dear family.

If the obvious injustices and hardships of many people's lives can be alleviated, there will be all the greater need for a more general and ungrudging recognition that fulfilment for oneself and for the people who depend upon one takes many valid forms. Just to get out of the habit of thinking that 'work' means 'paid job', and stop counting housewives as women who 'don't work', would allow some women to feel better about their lives. It could be a help too if people who write books about child care, who generally are careful to point out the diversity of children, also made a special effort to avoid stereotyping mothers as people with plenty of time if only they would allow themselves to relax and enjoy their babies. It is not only work outside the home or in it, but the pressing needs of the rest of the family, which disrupt this lovely ideal. It is easy to induce guilt and defensiveness in mothers who want to do their best for everyone and deeply feel that they are to blame for every imperfection.

LOOKING AT LANGUAGE

To think of women as oppressed is itself a stereotype. One thing is clear, that for good or ill many women have become more aware of themselves and their rights in recent years. As the liberation theologians put it, their consciousness has been raised. To some people, such development is long overdue; others persist in brushing feminist concern with language aside as rather silly. Granted that nowadays a woman can certainly be a chairman, is it an obvious corollary or an unnecessary piece of literal-mindedness to call her by the ugly name of 'chairperson'? Some people still need a good deal of persuading that it matters to take up saying 'humanity' instead of 'mankind'. Prejudice on both sides has ready-made answers about whether men and women will be happier or less happy for their increased awareness. If they sometimes seem to be more at odds with one another, less inclined to put up with each other's irritating ways, more prone to divorce and less able to offer stability to their children, do they need to return to tradition or take courage for a time of transition?

The whole question has become a sort of riding-school for hobby-horses. The ground is so trampled that the problems that matter are obscured. Before everyone loses patience with the evident bigotry of extremists on either side, clarification is needed rather than slogans. The language we use is shaped by, and in turn shapes, the notions we have about how the world is. Ordinary ways of speaking do influence the way people understand men and women and their roles, not least in marriage. When we gather together to celebrate the joining of a man and a woman in holy matrimony, the assumptions everyone concerned is making about what men and women are will matter for the meaning of the consent they give.

To insist correctly that 'man' in English includes woman, when it is the equivalent of the Latin *homo* rather than *vir*, makes no allowance for the effect that language has upon attitudes of mind. What has been called the 'invisibility' of women in ordinary speech about human beings has, over the centuries, built up men's self-confidence at the expense of women's. It is wishful thinking to suppose that women have really been included all the time. The only people who are likely to refer to an unborn baby as 'he' are the ones whose hearts are set upon a son and heir. Otherwise they will fall back upon the impersonal 'it', because they know that 'he' leaves out the possible 'she'. Nobody would say of Elizabeth Fry or Florence Nightingale, 'She was a great man'. There is still enormous resistance to the idea that a woman can represent at the holy table the Lord who was made man. 'He' does generally mean 'he', and 'man' calls up a picture in most people's minds of men. To find acceptable ways of restoring the balance we need more flexibility of mind and tongue than many of the contestants have shown so far. To ruin our language to do justice to women, to go about saying continually 'he or she' or 'everyone wants their rights', to stop appreciating large chunks of good English poetry, to admit that we no longer 'speak the tongue that Shakespeare spake': all this is just to replace one kind of destructive insensitivity by another.

Human language develops in any case and like Canute we know perfectly well that it is pointless to try to halt it. To use 'man' to mean 'people' is ceasing to be correct English. But the meanings of words do not simply develop on their own apart from human decisions, and there is a lot to be won or lost by the decisions being made now, decisions about how to live, about suggesting to other people how they should live and about describing how we and other people live. The enterprise which goes by the name of 'upholding family values', properly understood, is as needful but not as straightforward as some traditionalists suppose, since neither life nor language stays put to be defended, so that before we can uphold values we have to keep finding and elucidating them.

THE LANGUAGE OF THEOLOGY

Much of traditional Christianity has taken for granted the language of hierarchy. Husbands have been the rightful lords of their wives, though they were not supposed to 'lord it' over them. Nowadays it is the language of equality which is taken for granted more than we sometimes realize. At least in Christians' mental picture of how things are, a husband and a wife are both children of God. There are biblical foundations for both emphases, and people whose religious loyalty is much bound up with biblical authority can find confirmation in Gospels and Epistles for the pattern they prefer.

If we are honest about the whole tendency of our tradition through the centuries it has to be admitted that it is hierarchy which has prevailed. For wives to be obedient to their husbands has generally seemed quite unproblematic in theory, however it might be modified by the bossiness or charm, the weakness or generosity, of individual women or men. Some Christians would accept this tradition; and some, it has to be admitted, would rejoice in it. Feminists who want to stay in the Church can explain it, tolerantly in terms of social conditions which no longer apply, more fiercely by the continuing recalcitrance of dominating men.

There is no need to underestimate the possibilities of married happiness on either assumption, the hierarchical or the egalitarian. On the one hand women have experienced the security of knowing their duty; and on the other hand they are increasingly coming to enjoy the opportunity to work out their own salvation in loving co-operation with their husbands. There is a large unsolved problem, because most husbands and wives are not at present in a position either to live unselfconsciously by one or the other view or to make a plain choice between them. Many people today are obliged to live with a confusion of the two sets of ideas, because we are in transition.

It is at least clear that we have left behind the simple authority of husbands. Women have to 'come of age'. But if they are Christians, is this really in order? The hierarchical language of St Paul is not the point. Women who have given up wearing veils may surely give up treating their husbands as fathers, various quotable proof-texts[2] notwithstanding. But patriarchal notions are more deeply built into Christianity than that.

For Christians concerned with the relations between men and women, among all the slogans and stereotypes a question has to be faced. Is it possible both to believe in the God of the Bible and also to take feminist concerns seriously? Because we call God Father, does it follow that men really are more godlike than women, and that Christian family life should somehow reflect this idea? Is Christianity essentially for better or worse a patriarchal religion, not just in the way it happens to have developed but in its very nature? If it turns out that calling God 'Father' prevents us from recognizing the basic equality of women and men in God's sight, then our understanding of either God's Fatherhood or the equality of men and women, or both, must give way or undergo modification. Some would insist on the primacy and headship of men to the point of practically denying to women a share in the image of God; others would begin to call God 'Mother'; and both these would-be answers give offence.

Christians, like Jews, have been taught to look on the idea of a goddess as blasphemous, as a polytheistic rival to the one God. They have too easily deduced that men are more worthy than women to represent divinity. It is hard to eradicate the notion that there is something positively unworthy, inadequate or impure, about women in general. Honour paid to one woman, the virgin mother of the Lord, has even strengthened this impression. The argument more often deployed today, that men are not so much morally better as godlike in taking the initiative, proves mainly that prejudice is full of ingenuity.

Women are being told, both that there is no need to change our language because the masculine includes the feminine, and that it is wrong to change our language because masculine and feminine are not interchangeable. These arguments count against each other, but do they have any force separately?

Because in practice the masculine has not adequately included the feminine, there is a lot to be said for making more effort not to think of our God as exclusively male. There are images in the Bible, Old Testament and New, which redress the balance a little, including Deutero-Isaiah's 'I have made, and I will bear; I will carry and will save'[3] and the saying of Christ, 'How often would I have gathered your children together as a hen gathers her brood under her wings!'[4] There is scant encouragement for people who suppose that they can confine the Almighty within any one form of human imagery. We must keep varying our pictures and parables if we are even to begin to have an idea of what God is like.

For Christians the best authorized image is Father. Is it disloyal to the teaching of Christ simply to substitute Mother if we feel like it? Is there even a disloyalty, once we have seen harm in patriarchal language, about still feeling cautious? This is where the argument comes in that our imagery is not simply interchangeable. We can add new ideas more profitably than we can cut time-honoured ideas out. There is plenty of room for the enrichment of our religious language, especially perhaps by including images of birth and nourishment alongside forming and shaping in our idea of creation; but no room for impoverishment and reduction, for setting up Mother *against* Father. 'Parent' no doubt would avoid the unfairness of singling out one sex rather than the other; but who wants to address the God whom Jesus himself and the first Christians called Abba, Father, as Our Parent?

If women and men want to use 'Our Mother' as well as 'Our Father', they are embarking upon a complex adjustment of our imagery and it is quite fair to point out that this needs care. We could do with more emphasis on the creativity of women, rather than the dependence of children. Mother-and-baby is a powerful image for an intense stage in human parenthood which has to be outgrown. In demolishing female inadequacy and male headship, it would be odd to foster the notion that religion keeps us all infantile. Motherhood demands a series of separations: birth, weaning, sending into the world. As the children grow older, the roles of father and mother get more alike. The maternal separations are by no means goodbyes. Each in turn makes possible a more mature and more satisfying parental relationship. All this could have much to say about the grace of God and human freedom, which overemphasis upon the properly possessive early stages of motherhood could spoil.

If some women feel it hurtful that the Son also is male, and indeed when implications about the headship of men are drawn from the Incarnation, there are various ways of putting more emphasis upon the fully representative humanity of Christ and not going spinelessly along with a superficially patriarchal interpretation. People should stop understanding 'He was made man' as 'He was made male'. Jesus of Nazareth was indeed a man not a woman: this is a practical aspect of the 'scandal of particularity'. What matters for Christians is that he was a human being. It stands out in the accounts of his life that he treated women as people in a rare and encouraging way.[5] He did not choose a woman apostle: but how many Gentile apostles did he choose? Of course he is Head of the Church, and the Church is sometimes personified as female. It does not therefore make much sense to apply St Paul's arguments on these lines[6] in any direct way to twentieth-century husbands and wives; or indeed to be anxious because this early Christian way of thinking does not seem to give men and women today any particular help with their practical problems.

Christian feminists can, of course, put a good deal of weight on first-century practicalities. There is no need to jump to the conclusion that male 'headship' is the will of God for all time, and that the emancipation of women is a dangerous accommodation to secular thought. If men and women today find themselves able to reshape some traditions and become less hierarchical in their relationships, belief in Jesus Christ need not put difficulties about loyalty in their way.

COMPLEMENTING

There are two platitudes, one everyday and the other more theoretical, which come easily into the argument hereabouts to sort out problems about men's and women's roles in married life. The everyday idea is that what people need in marriage is 'give and take'; and this may turn out to be the more use of the two, especially if it is sometimes put the other way round as 'take and give'.

The grander notion is that men and women are supposed to be 'complementary' to one another. This is evidently true in a way, but itself needs some sorting out and qualification. 'Complementarity' as such is not as useful as we might hope because it represents several incompatible emphases; and the more carefully and courteously it is used, the more it is apt to cover up disagreements rather than resolve them.

When 'unisex' feminism was fashionable it was almost an insult to announce that women and men were complementary to one another. What women, or some women, were wanting was to be interchangeable with men, to have the same rights as men and not to be thought of as a different sort of creature. They aspired to be set free from family life and enter the world of men on equal terms. To call a woman 'feminine' seemed to have become objectionable. To affirm the 'complementarity' of male and female seemed not much better. Are women 'just as good' as men but with different virtues, gentleness and kindness instead of energy and fairness? 'Separate but equal' is not a phrase with a happy history.[7] 'Complementarity' can be too easily used as a palliative. It politely offers to encourage women and make them feel appreciated without modifying the practical dominance of men.[8]

The picture is more confused today, since some feminists seem to be reclaiming the assumptions upon which complementarity is based. They take their stand precisely upon the conviction that women are different: less fiercely competitive, more interested in people, less coolly rational; more, so to say, 'sisterly'. Instead of claiming 'equality' with men, the main feminist concern is to take account of women's experience.[9] Women's wants after all are found to be different from men's wants; but they no longer appreciate the double-edged chivalry with which men have prided themselves on honouring the weaker sex. It is not altogether a caricature to say that some articulate women see men neither as protectors to be admired, nor yet as colleagues to be emulated, but as oppressors who have kept women in subjection and prevented their human fulfilment. Instead of trying to escape from the family some women want to have it to themselves and exclude men.

What we cannot do with the idea of complementarity is use it as a slogan in this debate. It silences no opposition. It is quite likely to feed existing prejudices. There are the people on the one hand who consciously or unconsciously want to use it as a civil way of denigrating women, and feel a little aggrieved when women do not take complementarity as complimentary. There are other people who are just as willing to denigrate men and are happy to put them in their place by denying them the gentler virtues. There is all the more need for people who are repelled both by anti-feminism and by radical feminism to consider how we can understand and express whatever 'complementarity' ought to mean. Is it still an idea that we can use?

It does not follow that people who have outgrown subjection must want unisex and deny all natural differences between men and women. Nor does it follow that people who acknowledge differences must use them against one another. What is a good Christian feminism, or rather humanism, which will allow men and women thoroughly to respect and indeed love each other? War between the sexes is civil war. Sexual hostility does not just mark a frontier where we might eventually settle down in neutrality: it strikes precisely where we cannot, in the end, do without interdependence.

Maybe it would be a good plan to give the idea of complementarity a rest and let the notion of reciprocity do some of the work. Reciprocity is more dynamic and less inclined to suggest stereotypes. It allows for the 'twofoldness' of human beings, without the implication that the likeness or unlikeness of men and women is the most interesting question about them. Masculinity and feminity are not just two pre-existing roles to be accepted or refused. They are capacities to develop complex patterns. Just because people are not all one sort of interchangeable unit, it does not follow that instead they are simply two sorts of interchangeable unit.

'Complementarity' does not have to be phased out altogether. There remains a way in which men and women are complementary to one another, which is the foundation of their particular reciprocal relationships. Their fundamental complementarity is physical. Both liberals and traditionalists ought to feel encouraged by this plain statement. Liberals ought to feel set free, not forced on to the defensive, because it is distinctly limited. Complementarity does not need to be a matter of men being strong and women weak, men being assertive and women gentle, men being active and women passive. It is a matter of the way men's and women's bodies have evolved for the begetting, conceiving, bearing and nourishing of human young. There may be a tendency for 'masculine' and 'feminine' characteristics to arise, historically, out of the biological natures of men and women; but the rigid moral 'oughts' which have been assumed to arise from the biological 'is' have been misleading. If some women are tough and some men are meek, neither men nor women need be abashed or triumphant.

On the other hand traditionalists can be encouraged too by the assertion that the complementarity of men and women is a matter of their biological natures. Whatever else one wants to say about sexual ethics, the concept of marriage as a 'one-flesh union' has its basis in the physical compatibility of a man and a woman. Marriage is not just sexual relationship institutionalized. It is the joining of the lives of a man and a woman, intending permanence and characteristically with the hope of creating a family.

What about the joining of lives of people of the same gender? There is much more to be said about homosexuality; but the arguments are too tangled to be slipped in to a book about marriage. The refusal even to consider what possibilities ought to be available to homosexual people, their persecution by people who are able unthinkingly to count themselves as 'normal', has not been a good advertisement for traditional morality. Traditional morality ought to listen more carefully, both to married people themselves, and also to people who cannot be spouses. It ought to reform itself in sensitivity; but not in its definition of what marriage means.[10] To define marriage in terms of lifelong union between a man and a woman takes care of the complementarity. There is plenty of room for asking further questions about how marriage can best contribute to human happiness, and about how to avoid making victims either of people denied marriage altogether, or of people who enter into would-be lifelong unions and find themselves defeated.

The advantage of letting 'complementarity' do this somewhat limited job as part of the definition of marriage, and then bringing in the idea of reciprocity when we come to ask about the day-to-day relationships of men and women, is that reciprocity gives the flexibility we need at the stage where we need it. What 'reciprocity' means, put simply, is 'give and take',[11] beginning with the ordinary prosaic sense of that phrase. When two people live together life will be intolerable unless they can make adjustments and sometimes be capable of giving way without a fuss. But also they need to be able to reverse the order and discover what it means first to receive and then to reciprocate by giving; which is not exactly the same thing as 'paying back' but is near to the meaning of what Christians call 'grace'. It is a matter of being neither too proud to take nor too legalistic to give.

Husbands and wives who believe, consciously or unconsciously, in giving and taking more than they believe in pre-ordained masculine and feminine roles, have scope for working out together their own styles of living and loving. They need not therefore be deprived of the support they may receive from the traditions to which they belong. If the obligations they find themselves taking on seem to follow quite straightforwardly from the promises they have chosen to make to one another, the resulting simplicity need be neither naïve nor boring. But if, as may be a more frequent pattern nowadays, they find they have to make more decisions about who does what and how to shape their lives, then it is they, and of course their children, who will have the right to say in the end whether they have done well or ill.

Few plans are good or bad all of a piece. Most decisions have to be 'made good' by quite long processes of trying, adjusting and maturing. Other people can help, but not by insisting on the relevance of their own experience, however satisfactory. The problems, old and new, of harmonizing interests rather than over-riding them, are better solved by encouragement than by extraneous vetos. That is how unity can be developed out of the raw material of important and unimportant practical questions. A dance, old-time or modern, is a better image than a blueprint.

If a husband and wife decide together that the wife shall be the breadwinner while the husband looks after the children; if they divide the domestic chores evenly or unevenly between them; if they give up good jobs to live the simple life, or make what is perhaps a still more difficult decision to give up an experiment they have tried even if it has been a success; if they abandon convention or return to it: they are answerable to God and to their dependants, but not to people who have pet theories about human life and human roles.

The language of reciprocity is a long way from the language of rights, though it cannot get started if rights have been treated too roughly. It has a good deal to do with generosity, not as a sacrifice but as the 'harvest of the spirit': in other words, coming without realizing it to want what somebody else wants, so that giving and taking are not really distinct any more. If two lives are to be joined in anything like the way two lovers hope, such reciprocity is a necessary, and not unrealistic, condition. The reciprocity of marriage is fostered by the physical complementarity of a man and a woman; and it is capable of including, as a small part of its meaning, the ordinary sense of 'complementarity' in which two people have distinctly different gifts to offer to each other.

– 12 –
Marriage in context

What you sow does not come to life unless it dies.

1 Corinthians 15.36

GOOD FRIENDS

Is talking about reciprocity any more than a grandiose way of saying that a husband and wife should be friends? It was brought into the argument to introduce some flexibility into the notion of married people complementing each other. The biological difference between the sexes is neither to be ignored nor presumed upon. Being a man, or being a woman, leaves a lot to be worked out about our social roles; and the idea of reciprocity emphasizes that the working out is to be done together. Traditional headship is not even ruled out, provided that the exacting Pauline description of it is taken with rare seriousness.[1] So we come to speak of a sort of give and take based on contrast and likeness.

But friendship too is well described in this sort of way: so why should reciprocity be supposed to have a special relevance to marriage? With a little care one can take hold of this criticism, and instead of being much concerned to rebut it, make it the foundation of what remains to be said. Suppose reciprocity belongs in marriage just because marriage at its best depends upon friendship and cannot be properly understood without it?

There is some disentangling to be done to avoid some characteristic twentieth-century muddles about love and friendship. Freud's lesson that human beings are sexual beings has been well and truly taken to heart, though it is a pity to be so dazzled by it that we cannot see anything else. Meantime liberal Christians are glad to have learnt the lesson of the importance of 'personal relationships', which are sometimes taken to mean almost the same as love. It is partly insight, partly confusion, to try to add these two ways of thinking up to an enlightened Christian conclusion by making the double affirmation that human relationships are fundamentally sexual, and that good sexual relationships need stability. So marriage, which provides the necessary stability, can be glorified as the supreme example of personal relationship. One hopes in this way to be traditional and modern at the same time. A good deal of naïvety about men's and women's dealings with one another can be suitably avoided, and a good many worthwhile things can be said about the relationships of husbands and wives, but the price to be paid is quite heavy. Not only is the notion of celibacy hard to fit into this scheme; but because people are determined to show themselves unafraid of sexuality, they become unable to value any friendship which lacks overtly sexual expression.

So friendship comes to be thought of as just a kind of cooled-down 'love', filling a gap when people have not arrived at real, adult, sexual relationships. Children have 'best friends' much as they keep rabbits in hutches. People are 'just good friends' when they are drawing back from being 'in love'. We 'befriend' the lonely and unfortunate, who are missing real 'personal relationships'.

Then with good but confused intentions some religious people demote friendship in another way by treating it, not as cooled-down sex, but as warmed-up neighbourliness. 'Friendship' and 'fellowship' become almost synonymous, and in some current church usage both are shadows of what they could mean. The biblical concept of fellowship is enfeebled to mean hardly more than politeness, and friendship is tethered to it because of a sort of fear of real friendship which makes favourites.[2]

But real friendship is more important than these misunderstandings allow it to be. It is not something to make do with or to fall back upon. For human beings it is an end in itself rather than a means to some other end, whether sexual, economic, political or even religious. It enhances other relationships just because it has its own reality. Friendship is more than friendliness, though friendly people are ready to make friends. It is the particular and mutual appreciation of another man or woman as that very man or woman, not just as another person in general. Friendship shows itself primarily in the enjoyment of one another's company. Helping one's friends, or being helped by them, is secondary to affectionate communication.

Once all this has been said about friendship, it can then be happily applied to marriage as the characteristic sort of friendship which the human pairbond has developed. Having said that marriage is the joining of the lives of a man and a woman, we can explain that what makes sense of their choosing to belong to each other, including their physical union, is their mutual individual valuing of each other. If, the other way round, we try to characterize all personal relationships in terms of sexuality, we may be able to say all sorts of good things about marriage, but other kinds of friendship are left looking like sexual relationships deprived of sex.

When friendship is not given significance in its own right we shall miss opportunities for human happiness, and exaggerate unhappy trends. There will be less spontaneity in expressing all kinds of human affections for fear of stereotyped sexual assumptions. All warm relationships will tend towards one model, tyrannical if it becomes a monopoly. There will be more marriages based entirely upon physical attraction rather than upon liking. There will be more isolation of young couples as all in all to each other. Homosexual people will find themselves more typecast. There will be more pressure on people, young or older, to rate themselves according to their sexual prowess.

Now that people are becoming so concerned about the divorce rate and are wondering, often vainly, whether better marriage preparation would be the way to bring it down, it is worth pointing out that just as growing up with happily married parents is more use than any number of educational courses, so growing up knowing what friendship means is a similar kind of strong basis.

The best time to educate people for marriage is long before they are old enough to understand it. The time when the parents who gave them birth are no longer their whole world, and the people they will fall in love with are somewhere in the future, has been called the 'latency phase'. But human relationship is far from latent. They are busily entering into a heritage of human communication, and especially they are discovering what it is to make friends. They are loving and fickle, vulnerable and resilient. They are developing a capacity which can enhance the rest of their lives and bring them enjoyment, solace, encouragement and delight. They are learning about loyalty and disloyalty, co-operation and rivalry, patience and impatience, sympathy and envy, in what we hope are reasonably manageable doses. Older people can help by giving all this the importance it deserves. Friendship can be learnt as young as speech. We need not think of it as any more childish than language. If we want a good foundation for faithful marriage we can look here.

UNCOMFORTABLE WORDS

All this is a twentieth-century change of emphasis but hardly a revolution. What is still important is not to let one's enthusiasm for constructive changes of emphasis divert attention for ever from old questions which have not yet been properly faced. To drift out of one's tradition is less exciting than to renounce it, but may come to much the same thing in the end.

What needs to be faced, before an understanding of marriage which is both liberal and traditional can thoroughly come into its own, is the persistent negative strand in Christian teaching about sexuality. Honesty demands that this strand should not just be forgotten, and common sense insists that it will not simply go away if it is ignored.

The liberal hope for flexibility in our understanding of human relationships, which was how reciprocity came into the discussion, is far from being a traditional hope. There is an oddity, almost amounting to perversity, about the way flexibility is supposed to be applied. Various alternatives to traditional monogamous marriage are on offer: cohabitation, homosexual love, feminist rejection of the pairbond as oppressive, remarriage after divorce. Most of these the Christian Church has regarded as sinful, but we try nowadays to be more tolerant in our dealings with them all. Meantime there remains another alternative, more traditional and less fashionable: celibacy, which the Church has often treated with more honour than marriage. It certainly constitutes a gap in the argument so far.

Loyalty to the Christian tradition suggests that a Christian account of marriage should really be completed by a favourable account of celibacy as a parallel vocation: no longer supposed to be better than marriage, but still with an acknowledged validity of its own. The demand for an equally fair theological account of both vocations would be less reasonable than it sounds. With all goodwill, one is likely to misunderstand, or politely to idealize, the way that is not one's own.

Does the omission matter at all? Plenty of married Christians, especially Protestant Christians, would think that it does not matter, and even that it is preferable to forget about celibacy or minimize it. But surely it is right at least to feel regret at finding uncongenial what one's fellow human beings have found good. In any case for Christians to cut themselves off from this tradition is to cut themselves off from a large part of the Communion of Saints. As A. M. Allchin once pointed out, there may be 'important things to which our age is blind'.

Therefore a little more needs to be said: not to attempt an impossible overall view of both vocations, but to look at the vocation one knows in friendly awareness that it is not the only good way for human beings. The celibate way may be ignored or belittled rather than gratefully appreciated by married people partly because it makes them feel anxious; and the anxiety is not merely prejudice but has a theological base. How, in the providence of God, can it ever have been possible for the Church as a whole to take up such thoroughly negative attitudes towards sexuality as for centuries it undoubtedly did? There is a recent book by Professor Peter Brown[3] which goes far to make comprehension more possible. He enters with illuminating historical understanding into the positive ideas of the Christians of the first few centuries who were responsible for this tradition of sexual renunciation. In particular the Desert Fathers and St Augustine come to life, so that a great deal of the incomprehension, and indeed blaming, of these formative Christians which goes on in the Church today becomes less necessary.

A sadness remains which is not, as much as one had feared, for our predecessors' attitudes to the human body or to women, nor that they could not acknowledge marriage as good and God-given. The sadness is rather for the long absence from our tradition of the idea that the physical relationship between husband and wife is important for their developing unity. There is plenty of emphasis in the story on married Christians. They dutifully beget children, and indeed they enjoy the pleasures of sex, or they decide amicably to live in continence. But their love for one another seems brotherly and sisterly, without the thought that it could be nourished by their 'making love' to one another. The 'ends of marriage' are all allowed for, procreation, the right ordering of sexuality and companionship; but it seems as if these can almost be separated out in a way which does not do justice to what unity between a man and a woman can mean.

There is no reason why our century should not be allowed to make its own discoveries, and even maybe claim the guidance of the Holy Spirit for fresh insights. What is called, in ugly but useful jargon, 'the relational aspect of sex' is an emphasis of our times, and of course reliable contraception has had a good deal to do with it. We have some right to say that what we are now doing is appropriating the idea of the 'one-flesh union' and understanding it, at long last, as a real union of two lives which is both physical and spiritual.[4] But still it must be admitted that the weight of the contrary emphasis all down the Christian centuries is strong; and, more serious, that after all the negative emphasis is partly biblical in origin. Here is the heart of the problem of the Christian Church's attitude to sexuality.

If, within the Christian Church, the commendation of the honourable estate of marriage, as much more than a way of populating the world, still claims one's loyalty, there is work to be done to come to terms with some aspects of the biblical tradition itself. The celibacy of the Lord himself can be seen as needful for his work but not relevant to the marriage or celibacy of his followers; but the ready acceptance in the Church of belief in his mother's virginity does not make today's positive attitudes towards sexuality so simple as one would wish. Again, the tradition that he preached celibacy for some people 'for the sake of the kingdom of heaven'[5] can mean just that, but the tradition that according to his teaching there is no marriage in heaven since we shall all be 'as the angels'[6] is harder to fit into a coherent whole with what Christians believe about the value of marriage on earth. It is all very well to brush aside proof-texts. We need not suppose, either conveniently or inconveniently, that we have the very words of the Lord.[7] But if we find some features of his portrait as drawn in the Gospels hard to comprehend, surely more difficult than what we know of his attitude to divorce, it is imperative to give this part of the picture some attention.

In the Old Testament marrying and giving in marriage were held in high honour as the way to obey God's command to be fruitful and multiply and replenish the earth. Christian theologians, Catholic and Protestant,[8] have pointed out that Christ 'relativized' that command by announcing the coming of the Kingdom, thereby setting up celibacy too as a valuable vocation. Ought married and unmarried Christians alike to be perfectly content at this? It is surely not ungrateful for Christians who have found marriage good for its own sake to long for some stronger affirmation than permission to populate a now over-populated world. If fruitfulness were the whole meaning of marriage, of course marriage would be irrelevant and pointless in the Kingdom. Must that be the whole story? Must we tell Darby and Joan that they must look forward to a time when they will not belong to each other any more than to everybody else?

SO LONG AS YE BOTH SHALL LIVE . . .

To start arguing at once about life in heaven would be special pleading of a kind which succumbs to fundamentalism. It is more constructive for married Christians who are not biblical scholars to stand back from trying to interpret particular sayings and remember that the ground of all Christian hopes is resurrection, not immortality. We have to let go, but the promise is that the letting go is not to be the end. The kingdom has to do with death and rebirth, not with going on just as we are.

The hard sayings at least make us pause to ask the question whether marriage, not only celibacy, can be overemphasized by enthusiasts. When one thinks of some of the cruelties inflicted by

112

human beings upon one another in the name of the marriage bond, this question almost answers itself. People have been married against their will for reasons of state or family tradition. They have sometimes been compelled to remain married for no apparent benefit but the maintenance of the bond once tied. Women in particular have been vulnerable to a sort of life sentence of endless childbirth or miscarriage from which the only way out has too often been an early death. Whatever other vocations or indeed ambitions, or even just interests, they have wanted to have could be brushed aside. Meanwhile, when society at large has a moral certainty that all this is right, a whole range of possible unhappiness is created for people who find themselves unable to meet such demands. Infertility or inability to find a mate take on the extra burden of shame to add to disappointment. Marriage considered as if it were the only good, to which all else must be sacrificed, is as liable to be tyrannical as the contrary intolerance of natural human desires. Happily married people need to think about all this sometimes and understand that throughout human history there have been people who would be glad to be assured that it will not all be repeated in heaven.

The account of the creation of human beings in the first chapter of Genesis, 'male and female created he them',[9] is sometimes interpreted by theologians nowadays as if it were mainly about the creation of married couples. For instance D. S. Bailey's line of argument in his wise and formative book *The Man–Woman Relation in Christian Thought*[10] does not keep entirely clear of this trap. The more thankful one is for such a positive emphasis, as correcting the persistent blaming of all human troubles upon Eve the temptress, the more one needs to realize that couples are no more to be idolized than individuals.

We need to be able to say that marriage and the family are excellent but not absolute. We can take the hard saying about the resurrection, not as something wholly opaque which we can only hope distorts the teaching of the Lord, but as a salutary reminder that family life is not the same thing as the Kingdom.[11] We can certainly try to give up the hurtful way in which some Christians talk about 'Christian family life', as if the nuclear family of father, mother and children, were the centre of the Gospel: whereas on the contrary it seems clear that the Lord was quite critical of family demands. Even when the emphasis on 'the Christian family' is supposedly broadened to mean the Church, the same rather narrow set of domestic values is tacitly favoured in a way which makes many good people feel needlessly uncomfortable.

Can we do anything positive with the hard saying itself? At least we can be sure that if the Lord talked about angels in this or any

113

other context, the picture he intended to summon up in his hearers' imaginations would have been robust not flimsy. One might suggest, not too solemnly, that the much-maligned schoolmen speculating about each angel being unique could have more illumination for us than the imagery that comes into our minds of pious prettiness or engagingly under-rehearsed Nativity plays. But if we must have a proof-text to govern our thought about the next world, much the safest is 'You know neither the scriptures nor the power of God'.[12] Why should we jump to the conclusion that the transformation which our sexual natures need in the eyes of God must be to something less than the best we know in this life?

We have one positive clue in our experience. We already have an example of what it can mean for a special relationship to be outgrown but not lost. Being a mother or a father, in one sense, is a temporary role. In another sense, one's parents are one's parents for ever. The special character of the friendship which can develop between grown-up people who have been children and parents is sometimes one of the most rewarding aspects of human life. At its best it is enhanced by plenty of happy memories, but it does not have to live on memories: it is a going concern.

The dependence of children is over, but parenthood has not simply disappeared. Even the dependence has hardly disappeared into total independence. Affectionate human beings need each other more than that. Nor is parenthood going to lose its distinctive character and be transformed into the symmetrical kind of friendship we have with contemporaries. Its remaining characteristic asymmetry is what may give such poignancy to the role reversal of helpless old age.

When families have grown up, the question 'Have you any children?' becomes ambiguous. Perhaps there could be a like ambiguity about the question whether we have husbands and wives in the Kingdom of heaven. If parenthood can continue, when its role is outgrown, as a special and recognizable kind of friendship, and we are able to see this satisfying transformation happening in the midst of fallible and sometimes chaotic human lives, we can surely trust the power of God to raise up even more satisfying transformations of all the roles into which we put our hearts.

The Christian Gospel has plenty to say about giving up and receiving again. Whatever reason we have for believing the Gospel is reason for believing that the receiving again is to be even more real than the giving up. Eternal life is surely more than an insubstantial shadow of life on earth.

114

Appendix on the English divorce law

To see where we are going and where we ought to try to go, we need some understanding of how we have come to where we are. It is widely supposed that the history of the divorce law in England is a history of increasing permissiveness, the Christian Church giving way step by step to secular attitudes, and partly betrayed by trendy liberals in its midst. The truth, as usual, is more complicated. The development of the English divorce law has been a matter of attempts by church people and others to improve on existing arrangements for coping with hardness of heart.[1] On the assumption that the Lord allowed divorce for adultery[2] it seemed unfair that this relief should be available only by private Act of Parliament to the rich and powerful. On the assumption that St Paul allowed divorce for desertion[3] it seemed unfair that only adultery could count when many other cases were equally hard. So on Christian responsibility, and supposedly on a basis of New Testament teaching, the matrimonial offence became the foundation of the divorce law of England.

What this meant was that in spite of themselves Christians came to be identified with the strange belief that loyalty to Christ required the prohibition of divorce unless one spouse had committed a particular kind of sin and the other refused to forgive. If neither party could be singled out as guilty, or if they both wanted the divorce, they were tied to each other for life, unless one of them was prepared to lie to the court. The resulting anomalies were notorious and nobody could have supposed that all this had much to do with the will of God.

So just as Christians had taken a main part in the making of the divorce law of England in the nineteenth century, they took a main part in its reform in the twentieth. A group of church people was appointed by the Archbishop of Canterbury to discuss, not theology, but what advice in this matter the Church could give to the state. The Divorce Law Reform Act of 1969 represented a partial acceptance by Parliament of the recommendations of the group's report, *Putting Asunder*.[4] Their concern that the divorce law should be less unjust was an attempt to find out what might be God's will for lawmakers, not a dishonest attempt to find ways round God's will for spouses. Their positive contribution was the concept that it is not assorted offences, which are generally merely symptoms, but the decisive breakdown of the union of husband and wife, which justifies the legal untying of the marriage bond. In this attempt to put the law of divorce upon a sounder footing they were partly successful and partly unsuccessful. Some conspicuous human misery has been dealt with at a cost which indeed may still be thought worth while, though it must be admitted that this cost was inadequately foreseen.

Developments since 1969 have tended to make divorce easier, cheaper and less important, and to get further from any idea that divorce is somebody's fault and that the maintaining of the marriage is somebody's responsibility. *Putting Asunder* argued that to insist upon specifying one innocent and one guilty party was intolerably artificial. From this has been developed as a kind of orthodoxy the 'no fault' doctrine, that blame at any stage is irrelevant and even pernicious, that anyone who is definitely unhappy in a marriage has a right to be divorced and try again, and that property is to be 'split down the middle' in almost all circumstances. If thinking Christians still believe that getting rid of the artificial dominance of the matrimonial offence was right, there is a lot of work to be done by a suitably chastened Christian liberalism, not to accept the necessity for a rigorist backlash, but to understand what has gone wrong and what after all has not gone wrong.

The Law Commission's discussion document *Facing the Future*[5] shows convincingly that quite a lot has gone wrong. It gives an only too convincing analysis of how the present law of breakdown, based on various 'facts' requiring various lengths of time to establish, is in a bad way. It is making divorce more painful and less honest than it need be, but not more unlikely. As in the old days people were more concerned to get their divorces than truly to prove offence, so now they are more concerned to get their divorces than truly to prove breakdown. Because they do not want to wait five years or even two years for divorce they will dredge up intolerable conduct or allege adultery, with no defence possible unless the divorce itself is to be contested. Grievances are summoned up that were hardly noticed at the time and come as a shock even to a respondent who is entirely willing to be divorced. All this does not offer much hope to children whose best hope for the future is that they will be given the chance to go on loving both parents. The responsible weight of these argu- ments should not be underestimated. They make a case, unpleasing as it may be to Christians, for acknowledging breakdown and granting divorce on the application of either spouse, after an interval of some months for the settling of 'ancillary matters' with the minimum of bitterness. The Scottish Law Commission has set out similar arguments, coming to the less radical conclusion that adultery and unreasonable behaviour should not disappear from the law, but that the separation periods should be considerably shortened.[6]

If this is the way things are moving, it seems that marriage must become increasingly like an ordinary contract which can be dissolved at the will of the parties, although for centuries the Church and the law have been in agreement that it is, on the contrary, a 'contract conferring status'. Not only in church but in register offices,[7] marriage has been plainly understood to be a lifelong commitment. Will it matter if this legal understanding of marriage is lost? At present people have available to them an option which is generally valued, of committing themselves to one another in a permanent way which can be expected to last. To abolish the reality of this option would be a heavy price to pay for relieving the admitted distresses of the present law of divorce.

Realism suggests that recognition of the public interest in stable unions cannot be built into the breakdown principle: it must somehow be superimposed upon it. At present there is a presump- tion, but a rebuttable presumption, that marriage is permanent. The presumption is rebutted if the marriage has broken down. But if breakdown is established by the bare word of one spouse, then the presumption of permanence is not merely rebutted in a particular case but destroyed. So the question which people who care about the stability of the marriage union ought to be asking is: could break- down in turn become, as it were, a rebuttable ground for divorce? Could some further condition for divorce be required, over and above the assertion of breakdown? *Putting Asunder* attempted such a qualification, hoping to answer the objection that breakdown on its own would disgracefully allow offenders to take advantage of their own wrong.[8] Now that the divorce law is widely agreed to need reforming again, it is surely time for further consideration of the unsolved problem of how not to allow more and more exceptions to destroy the norm.

Notes

Chapter 1 Where are we?
1 G. R. Dunstan, *The Family Is Not Broken* (SCM, 1962).
2 R. Fletcher, *Britain in the Sixties: the family and marriage* (Penguin, 1962); 3rd edition (Pelican, 1973) as just *The Family and Marriage*.

Chapter 2 The pairbond
1 (SPCK, 1971).
2 (Harvester Press, 1978), p. 304.
3 Ibid.
4 Mark 10.6–8.
5 D. Johanson and M. A. Edey, *Lucy: the beginnings of humankind* (Granada, 1981).
6 Ibid., chapter 16.
7 Terence, *Heauton Timorumenos*, 77.
8 Genesis 29.20.
9 1 Samuel 1.8.
10 See e.g. A. M. Allchin, 'The sacrament of marriage in Eastern Christianity', Appendix 3 of *Marriage, Divorce and the Church* (The Root Report; SPCK, 1971); Paul Evdokimov, *The Sacrament of Love* (St Vladimir's Seminary Press, 1985).
11 *St John Chrysostom on Marriage and Family Life* (St Vladimir's Seminary Press, 1986), Homily 20, p. 43.
12 Ibid., pp. 46–7.
13 *Scholar Extraordinary: the life of Professor the Rt Hon. Friedrich Max Müller, PC* (Chatto and Windus, 1974), p. 149.
14 Ibid., p. 151.
15 Ibid., p. 148.
16 (Methuen, 1963), p. 167.

Chapter 3 Fidelity
1 (April 1984), p. 243.
2 Psalm 15.5 (Book of Common Prayer).
3 September 1973.
4 (Darton, Longman and Todd, 1970), p. 90.
5 *Sense and Sensibility*, chapter 36.
6 *Othello* I:3 and III:3. It was from *The Moor of Venice* by Richard Flatter (Heinemann, 1950; pp. 70–1 and 87) that I learnt the importance of Iago's making Othello aware that Desdemona is capable of deceit.
7 'Performative utterances' in *Philosophical Papers* (Oxford, 1961); and *How to Do Things with Words* (1962), quoted in *Marriage, Divorce and the Church*, Appendix 5.
8 *Being and Having* (Dacre, 1949), p. 46.

Chapter 4 Exclusiveness
1 1981.
2 I come back to the question of the interpretation of Christ's teaching in Chapter 5, and to the question of remarriage in church in Chapter 9.
3 (Allen, 1984).
4 *The Man-Woman Relation in Christian Thought* (Longman, 1959 [Pelican, 1979]), pp. 131-3.
5 The rest of this paragraph comes from *The Marriage Bond*, p. 21.
6 The rest of this paragraph comes from *The Marriage Bond*, p. 47.

Chapter 5 Christian teaching
1 J. Barr, *The Bible in the Modern World* (SCM, 1973), p. 136. See also J. Barton, *People of the Book? The authority of the Bible in Christianity* (SPCK, 1988).
2 J. Barr, ibid., p. 112.
3 Cf. Helen Oppenheimer, *Incarnation and Immanence* (Hodder, 1973), pp. 91ff. and 'Making God findable' in *The Parish Church*, ed. Giles Ecclestone (Mowbray, 1988), p. 74.
4 J. Barr, ibid., p. 123.
5 C. F. Evans, *The Lord's Prayer* (SPCK, 1963), p. 12.
6 1 Thessalonians 5.9-11.
7 Romans 15.7.
8 Philippians 2.10.
9 1 Corinthians 7.15.
10 Matthew 5.32 and 19.9.
11 This paragraph comes from *The Marriage Bond*, p. 57.
12 Cf. *The Marriage Bond*, p. 58. The rest of this paragraph comes from *The Marriage Bond*, p. 60.

Chapter 6 Beyond fairness
1 Matthew 19.10.
2 Galatians 5.22-23.
See J. Jeremias, *The Sermon on the Mount* (Ethel M. Wood Lecture; Athlone Press, 1961) e.g. pp. 29-32: '. . . the gift of God precedes His demands'.
3 I have taken this sentence from my first book, *Law and Love* (Faith Press, 1962).
4 'For a marriage' in *A Celebration of Faith* (Hodder, 1970), p. 137.
5 This sentence comes from the *Modern Churchman* article, mostly used in Chapter 5 (1984, p. 28).
6 See J. Burgoyne, R. Ormrod and M. Richards, *Divorce Matters* (Pelican, 1986).
7 This paragraph and the next are based upon *The Marriage Bond*, pp. 32-3.
8 See above, p. 51.

Chapter 7 Sacrament
1 Articles of Religion, XXV.
2 The Catechism.
3 Ephesians 5.32.
4 See D. S. Bailey, *The Man-Woman Relation in Christian Thought*, pp. 114-15 and E. Schillebeeckx, *Marriage: secular reality and saving mystery* (Sheed and Ward, 1965) II, pp. 68-70.

5 E.g. Pope Pius XI at the beginning of *Casti Connubii*, 31.12.1930.

6 Introduction to the wedding service; cf. above, p. 8.

7 Mark 10.6ff.; see above, p. 9.

8 'For a marriage' (see Chapter 6, note 4).

9 *Church Dogmatics* III.4, I.128.

10 Cf. Helen Oppenheimer, Appendix 4 of *Marriage, Divorce and the Church*, 'Marriage as illustrating some Christian doctrines', reprinted in *Marriage and the Doctrine of the Church of England* (CUP, 1985), pp. 35-6.

11 The rest of this paragraph comes from *The Marriage Bond*, p. 28; and see ibid., p. 25, and *Incarnation and Immanence*, pp. 171-3.

12 Cf. pp. 53-4 above and *The Marriage Bond*, pp. 32-3.

13 Cf. *The Marriage Bond*, p. 29.

14 See E. Schillebeeckx, *Marriage: secular reality and saving mystery* I, p. 63.

15 Ephesians 5.21-33; cf. above, pp. 58, 60 and *The Marriage Bond*, p. 35.

16 See J. Gosling, *Marriage and the Love of God* (Geoffrey Chapman, 1965), especially the chapter called 'The use of the sacrament I'.

17 This paragraph is based on *The Marriage Bond*, pp. 33-4.

18 Cf. E. Schillebeeckx, *Marriage: secular reality and saving mystery* II, pp. 79, 91.

Chapter 8 Foundation fairness

1 Deuteronomy 24.

2 The rest of this section is based on *The Marriage Bond*, pp. 69-70. See also Helen Oppenheimer, *Law and Love*, chapter 3.

3 Matthew 19.8: Authorized Version.

4 Cf. *Law and Love*, pp. 73-4.

5 English Law Commission, 1966. See Law Commission Discussion Paper, *Facing the Future* (HM Stationery Office, 1988) section 3(a).

6 As recommended in *Putting Asunder: a divorce law for contemporary society*, the report of a group appointed by the Archbishop of Canterbury (SPCK, 1966).

7 *Facing the Future*, 2.17.

8 Ibid., 4.14.

9 Ibid., 5.20.

10 Ibid., 5.22-52.

11 See J. Burgoyne, R. Ormrod and M. Richards, *Divorce Matters* (Chapter 6, note 6 above), p. 60.

12 *The Enforcement of Morals* (Oxford, 1965), chapter 14, 'Morals and the law of marriage', p. 66.

Chapter 9 Holy wedlock

1 See *An Honourable Estate* (Report of the Working Party on the law of marriage set up by the General Synod; Church House Publishing, 1988) paras 177-83.

2 Much of this section is based on *The Marriage Bond*, pp. 26-7.

3 See e.g. Wesley Carr, *Brief Encounters* (SPCK, 1985); P. Chambers, *Made in Heaven?* (SPCK, 1988).

4 See above, pp. 45, 46.

5 See above, pp. 27-9.

6 1981.

7 At the end of *The Marriage Bond*.

Chapter 10 Parents and children

1 Cf. Helen Oppenheimer, *The Character of Christian Morality* (Faith Press, 2nd edition 1974), p. 23; and *The Marriage Bond*, p. 19.
2 See above, pp. 51, 54–6.
3 See above, p. 62.
4 Shakespeare: Sonnet 2.
5 Cf. Helen Oppenheimer, Appendix 4 of *Marriage, Divorce and the Church*, last section 'Marriage and creation' (see Chapter 7, note 10 above).
6 Traherne, *Centuries* 42.
7 Ephesians 4.13 (Authorized Version).

Chapter 11 Roles

1 E.g. Mary Midgley and Judith Hughes, *Women's Choices* (Weidenfeld and Nicolson, 1983); cf. *The Marriage Bond*, pp. 43–6.
2 E.g. 1 Corinthians 11.3–16, 14.34–35.
3 Isaiah 46.4.
4 Luke 13.34.
5 See Anne Primavesi and Jennifer Henderson, *Our God has No Favourites* (Burns & Oates, 1989).
6 E.g. in Ephesians 5.21–33.
7 *The Marriage Bond*, p. 45.
8 There is an agreeable discussion of 'complementarity' in J. Gosling, *Marriage and the Love of God*, pp. 152ff. He points out that women 'seem to lack the required mindless passivity', and goes on to suggest that husband and wife are not merely to be complementary parts of a team, permanently deploying different qualities, but are to encourage each other towards maturity.
9 See the article 'Feminist Ethics' in the *New Dictionary of Christian Ethics* (SCM, 1967).
10 See *Homosexual Relations: a contribution to discussion* (CIO, published for the C. of E. Board of Social Responsibility, 1979) e.g. para. 160; and Robert Runcie, 'Homosexuality' in *Windows onto God* (SPCK, 1983).
11 Cf. Helen Oppenheimer, 'Temperance' in *Traditional Virtues Reassessed*, ed. A. R. Vidler (SPCK, 1964).

Chapter 12 Marriage in context

1 Ephesians 5.21–33.
2 Cf. Helen Oppenheimer, *The Hope of Happiness* (SCM, 1983), pp. 134ff.
3 P. Brown, *The Body and Society: men, women and sexual renunciation in early Christianity* (Faber and Faber, 1989).
4 As D. S. Bailey put it, discussing the Genesis accounts of creation in *The Man-Woman Relation in Christian Thought* (p. 265): 'In the earlier (J) creation story the first human pair cleave together, not merely to procreate their kind, but to establish a relationship of such intimacy and significance that they are said to become one-flesh. In the later (P) source the personal and relational element is still further emphasized.'
5 Matthew 19.12.
6 Matthew 22.30.
7 See above, pp. 39, 41–2.
8 E.g. Barth, *Church Dogmatics* III. 4.1, pp. 143–4ff.; E. Schillebeeckx,

Marriage: secular reality and saving mystery I, pp. 180ff.; D. S. Bailey, *The Man-Woman Relation in Christian Thought*, p. 285.

9 Genesis 1.27.

10 D. S. Bailey, *The Man-Woman Relation in Christian Thought*, last chapter, especially pp. 271, 275-6.

11 Cf. Helen Oppenheimer, articles on 'Marriage' in *A New Dictionary of Christian Theology* (SCM, 1983), p. 347 and in *A New Dictionary of Christian Ethics* (SCM, 1986), p. 368; and *The Hope of Happiness*, p. 134.

12 Matthew 22.29.

Appendix

1 Cf. *The Marriage Bond*, pp. 70ff.; and see A. R. Winnett, *Divorce and Remarriage in Anglicanism* (Macmillan, 1958), chapter IX.

2 The so-called 'Matthaean exception': Matthew 5.32 and 19.9.

3 The so-called 'Pauline privilege': 1 Corinthians 7.15.

4 (SPCK, 1966).

5 (HM Stationery Office, 1988).

6 *Report on Reform of the Ground for Divorce* (H.M. Stationery Office, Edinburgh, 1989).

7 See above, pp. 1-2.

8 *Putting Asunder*, para. 66.

Some useful reading

Books

D. Atkinson, *To Have and to Hold* (Collins, 1979)

D. S. Bailey, *The Man–Woman Relation in Christian Thought* (Longman, 1959; Pelican, 1979)

J. Barton, *People of the Book? The authority of the Bible in Christianity* (SPCK, 1988)

B. and P. Berger, *The War over the Family: capturing the middle ground* (Pelican, 1983)

Anne Borrowdale, *A Woman's Work: changing Christian attitudes* (SPCK, 1989)

P. Brown, *The Body and Society: men, women and sexual renunciation in early Christianity* (Faber and Faber, 1989)

J. Burgoyne, R. Ormrod, and M. Richards, *Divorce Matters* (Pelican, 1986)

Wesley Carr, *Brief Encounters: pastoral ministry through the occasional offices* (SPCK, 1985)

P. Chambers, *Made in Heaven? Ministry with those intending marriage* (SPCK, 1988)

J. Dominian, *Sexual Integrity: the answer to AIDS* (Darton, Longman & Todd, 1987)

G. Duby, *The Knight, the Lady and the Priest: the making of modern marriage in medieval France* (Penguin, 1984).

P. Evdokimov, *The sacrament of love* (St Vladimir's Seminary Press, 1985)

R. Fletcher, *Britain in the sixties: the family and marriage* (Penguin, 1962; 3rd edition, as *The Family and Marriage*, Pelican, 1973)

Betty Friedan, *The Second Stage* (Michael Joseph, 1982)

J. R. Gillis, *For Better, for Worse: British marriages, 1600 to the present* (Oxford, 1985)

J. Gosling, *Marriage and the Love of God* (Geoffrey Chapman, 1965)

A. M. Greeley, *Love and Play* (W. H. Allen, 1984)

A. Hastings, *Christian Marriage in Africa: a report* (commissioned by the Anglican Archbishops; SPCK, 1973)

D. Johanson and M. A. Edey, *Lucy: the beginnings of humankind* (Granada, 1981)

St John Chrysostom on Marriage and Family Life (St Vladimir's Seminary Press, 1986)

Mary Midgley and Judith Hughes, *Women's Choices* (Weidenfeld and Nicolson, 1983)

125

E. Schillebeeckx, *Marriage: secular reality and saving mystery* (Sheed and Ward, 1965)

A. Soble (ed.) *Philosophy of Sex* (Rowman and Littlefield/Sheldon Press, 1980)

P. Turner (ed.) *Men and Women: sexual ethics in turbulent times* (Cowley Publications (USA), 1989)

A. R. Winnett, *Divorce and Remarriage in Anglicanism* (Macmillan, 1958)

A. R. Winnett, *The Church and Divorce* (Mowbray, 1968)

Pamphlets, articles and chapters

A. M. Allchin, 'The sacrament of marriage in Eastern Christianity', Appendix 3 of *Marriage, Divorce and the Church* (The Root Report; SPCK, 1971)

Karl Barth, *Church Dogmatics* III.1, 3, 4

John W. Bullimore, *Pushing Asunder?* (Grove Books on Ethics, 41; 1981)

N. C. Chaudhuri, *Scholar Extraordinary: the life of Professor the Rt Hon. Friedrich Max Müller, PC* (Chatto and Windus, 1974), Part 2, chapter 2

Patrick Devlin, *The Enforcement of Morals* (Oxford, 1965), chapter 14

Hugh Dickinson, 'Bound or free?', *Theology* (March 1986)

J. Dominian, *Marriage in Britain 1945-80* (Study Commission on the Family, 1980)

J. Dominian, *Families in the Future* (final report; Study Commission on the Family, 1983)

G. R. Dunstan, *The Marriage Covenant* (Cambridge University Sermon; CIO, 1961)

Austin Farrer, 'For a marriage' in *A Celebration of Faith* (Hodder, 1970)

J. Jeremias, *The Sermon on the Mount* (Ethel M. Wood Lecture 1961; Athlone Press, 1961)

Helen Oppenheimer, articles on 'Marriage' in *A New Dictionary of Christian Theology* (SCM, 1983), p. 347, and on 'Marriage' and 'Divorce' in *A New Dictionary of Christian Ethics* (SCM, 1986), p. 368

Philip Turner, *Divorce: a Christian perspective* (Forward Movement Publications [USA], 1983)

Reports

Putting Asunder: a divorce law for contemporary society (SPCK, 1966)

Marriage, Divorce and the Church (The Root Report; SPCK, 1971)

Marriage and the Church's Task (The Lichfield Report; CIO, 1978)

The House of Bishops Marriage Education Panel has published 'study extracts' from these two reports, under the title *Marriage and the Doctrine of the Church of England* (Cambridge University Press, 1985)

Homosexual Relations: a Contribution to Discussion (CIO, published for the C. of E. Board of Social Responsibility, 1979)

Marriage Matters (Home Office and DHSS; HM Stationery Office, 1979)

An Honourable Estate: The Doctrine of Marriage According to English Law: the obligation of the church to perform marriages (The report of a Working Party established by the General Synod of the Church of England; Church House Publishing, 1988)

English Law Commission, *Facing the Future* (HM Stationery Office, 1988)

Making Women Visible: the use of inclusive language with the ASB (Liturgical Commission; Church House Publishing, 1988)

Scottish Law Commission, *Report on Reform of the Ground of Divorce* (HM Stationery Office, Edinburgh, 1989)

Index